Ask
the Prophets

E. E. Cleveland

Ask the Prophets

Contents

Foreword

The Book

The Bible is the book for *today*. It contains answers to *today's* questions and solutions to *today's* problems. It relates to youth and old age, rich and poor. Its principles are eternal and its scope universal. History has verified its predictions, and archeology sustains its historical record. No scientific *facts* (in striking contrast with certain theories and speculations) refute its revelations, nor geology its conclusions. Doctrine, science, history, and prophecy adorn its sacred pages. Its words are charged with light and life. Its wisdom is pre-eminent in all the world. Give your attention to it, reader, for in it lies your only hope of spiritual abundance here and life in the world to come.

The Prophets

The Bible calls them holy men. This was true, not because they were naturally good, but because God placed upon them the high gift of grace, the gift of the Holy Ghost. Through them God chose to communicate His light to the world. These men were inspired in the sense that God told them what to say. The prophets were God's penmen, not His pen. What they wrote is therefore the inspired Word of God. These men were not infallible, but their revelations are. The prophets were human beings, but their messages have a divine source. Therefore, *you can trust the prophets.*

The Divinity of Christ

I

The Divinity of Christ

Jesus Christ is the crisis of history, for history is His story. Secular time is dated by Him. His foundational teachings are the basis of law in all civilized society. Infidels and atheists denounce Him. His followers extol Him. Around the world He is worshiped in sermon, song, and supplication.

He was born in a manger, and but for divine intervention He would have been murdered before He was two years old. At the age of twelve He displayed wisdom that amazed His superiors. They could not account for His knowledge and acumen. He was baptized by John at the Jordan, and entered upon His teaching ministry. It was His teaching, as well as His miracles, that brought Him into conflict with the religious leaders of Israel. This led ultimately to His horrible death at Golgotha, hill of skulls. He was buried in Joseph's tomb, but rose from the dead early the first day of the week, and ascended to God.

Who was He? His followers worshiped Him as God. His enemies said to Him, "Thou hast a devil." The multitude was divided concerning Him. What is the truth?

Question: **Moses, what assurance of a Redeemer did God make as He told Satan of his ultimate defeat?**
Answer: "And I will put enmity between thee and the woman, and between thy seed and her seed; it shall bruise thy head [a mortal wound], and thou shalt bruise his heel [a superficial wound]." Genesis 3:15.

Question: **Matthew, when was the Saviour's "heel" bruised?**
Answer: "And they crucified him." Matthew 27:35.

Question: **John, since Jesus Christ is divine, He must have lived long before His birth at Bethlehem. What did He say?**

10

Answer: "O Father, glorify thou me with thine own self with the glory which I had with thee before the world was." John 17:5.

Question: **How do you explain this, John?**

Answer: "In the beginning was the Word [Christ], and the Word was with God, and the Word was God." John 1:1.

Question: **John, when you say "the Word was God," how can we be sure that you speak of Jesus Christ?**

Answer: "The Word was made flesh, and dwelt among us, (and we beheld his glory, the glory as of the only begotten of the Father,) full of grace and truth." John 1:14.

Question: **I suppose that should settle it. You testify of what you saw. You were with Him. That is sufficient. Have you anything further to add?**

Answer: "The same was in the beginning with God." John 1:2.

Question: **Amazing! Then you believe that Christ, like God the Father, is eternal and therefore God. But to be divine He must have creative power. What about this?**

Answer: "All things were made by him; and without him was not any thing made that was made." John 1:3.

Question: **Paul, John has just made an amazing revelation. Do you agree with him?**

Answer: "For by him were all things created, that are in heaven, and that are in earth, visible and invisible, whether they be thrones, or dominions, or principalities, or powers: all things were created by him, and for him." Colossians 1:16.

Question: **Paul, did Christ exist before the world?**

Answer: "He is before all things, and by him all things consist." Colossians 1:17.

Question: **Thank you, Paul. Evolution certainly takes a beating here! Man did not come up from the slime pits, but was created by Jesus Christ. Wonderful! Luke, Paul says, "By him all things consist." What does he mean by that?**

Answer: "For in him we live, and move, and have our being; as certain also of your own poets have said, For we are also his offspring." Acts 17:28.

Question: **Isaiah, you spoke of the birth of Christ. Do you believe that He is divine?**

Answer: "For unto us a child is born, unto us a son is given:

11

and the government shall be upon his shoulder: and his name shall be called Wonderful, Counsellor, The mighty God, The everlasting Father, The Prince of Peace.'' Isaiah 9:6.

Question: **John, what did Jesus say of Himself?**
Answer: ''I am Alpha and Omega, the beginning and the ending, saith the Lord, which is, and which was, and which is to come, the Almighty.'' Revelation 1:8.

Question: **While He was on earth, was Jesus ever concerned that man should know His true identity? Matthew, have you an answer?**
Answer: ''When Jesus came into the coasts of Caesarea Philippi, he asked his disciples, saying, Whom do men say that I the Son of man am?'' Matthew 16:13.

Question: **Did all men understand just who He is?**
Answer: ''And they said, Some say that thou art John the Baptist: some, Elias; and others, Jeremias, or one of the prophets.'' Matthew 16:14.

Question: **When Christ pressed His own disciples as to their personal belief, who answered, Matthew, and what did he say?**
Answer: ''And Simon Peter answered and said, Thou art the Christ, the Son of the living God.'' Matthew 16:16.

Question: **In what words did Jesus indicate His agreement with Peter's conclusion?**
Answer: ''Jesus answered, and said unto him, Blessed art thou, Simon Barjona: for flesh and blood hath not revealed it unto thee, but my Father which is in heaven.'' Matthew 16:17.

Question: **John, on one occasion Jesus healed a man who had been blind from birth. What was the man's conclusion when he discovered Christ's divinity?**
Answer: ''He said, Lord, I believe. And he worshipped him.'' John 9:38.

Question: **What happened in the Temple at the Feast of Tabernacles that should have opened the people's eyes?**
Answer: ''In the last day, that great day of the feast, Jesus stood and cried, saying, If any man thirst, let him come unto me, and drink. He that believeth on me, as the scripture hath said, out of his belly shall flow rivers of living water.'' John 7:37, 38.

Question: **Even demons recognized Him as the Divine One. Is this not so, Luke?**

Answer: "In the synagogue there was a man, which had a spirit of an unclean devil, and cried out with a loud voice, saying, Let us alone; what have we to do with thee, thou Jesus of Nazareth? art thou come to destroy us? I know thee who thou art; the Holy One of God." Luke 4:33, 34.

Question: **Even the devil told the truth on this occasion. How did Jesus reveal His power over the devil?**

Answer: "Jesus rebuked him, saying, Hold thy peace, and come out of him. And when the devil had thrown him in the midst, he came out of him, and hurt him not." Luke 4:35.

Question: **Was there general agreement among the demons that Christ is divine?**

Answer: "Devils also came out of many, crying out, and saying, Thou art Christ the Son of God. And he rebuking them suffered them not to speak: for they knew that he was Christ." Luke 4:41.

Question: **I am not surprised that they knew Him, for He was their Creator. Also it was Christ who drove them out of heaven when they sinned. Luke, did Christ ever say anything about this in your hearing?**

Answer: "He said unto them, I beheld Satan as lightning fall from heaven." Luke 10:18.

Question: **John, you were given a detailed description of this encounter. How did it happen?**

Answer: "There was war in heaven: Michael and his angels fought against the dragon; and the dragon fought and his angels, and prevailed not; neither was their place found any more in heaven." Revelation 12:7, 8.

Question: **John, where were these evil angels driven?**

Answer: "The great dragon was cast out, that old serpent, called the Devil, and Satan, which deceiveth the whole world: he was cast out into the earth, and his angels were cast out with him." Revelation 12:9.

Question: **God ought to be able to raise the dead. Neither men nor angels can do so. Did Jesus ever do this?**

Answer: "When he [Jesus] thus had spoken, he cried with a

loud voice, Lazarus, come forth. And he that was dead came forth, bound hand and foot with graveclothes: and his face was bound about with a napkin. Jesus saith unto them, Loose him, and let him go.'' John 11:43, 44.

Question: **But was he** *really dead,* **John?**
Answer: "Martha, the sister of him that was dead, saith unto him, Lord, by this time he stinketh: for he hath been dead four days.'' John 11:39.

Question: **Only God could have raised Lazarus, John. How could Jesus do so?**
Answer: "In him was life; and the life was the light of men.'' John 1:4.

Question: **That is clear. In Him was life unborrowed, underived. Jesus Christ is God! Why was He willing to die for our sins, Paul?**
Answer: "God commendeth his love toward us, in that, while we were yet sinners, Christ died for us.'' Romans 5:8.

Question: **What a thought! He loves us; why else would He take our place in death? Were there witnesses to His burial?**
Answer: "When Joseph had taken the body, he wrapped it in a clean linen cloth, and laid it in his own new tomb, which he had hewn out in the rock: and he rolled a great stone to the door of the sepulchre, and departed. And there was Mary Magdalene, and the other Mary, sitting over against the sepulchre.'' Matthew 27:59-61.

Question: **What precautions did Pilate take to secure the tomb?**
Answer: "So they went, and made the sepulchre sure, sealing the stone, and setting a watch.'' Matthew 27:66.

Question: **Matthew, this is crucial. What happened early the next morning?**
Answer: "Behold, there was a great earthquake: for the angel of the Lord descended from heaven, and came and rolled back the stone from the door, and sat upon it.'' Matthew 28:2.

Question: **How did the angel explain this occurrence?**
Answer: "The angel answered and said unto the women, Fear not ye: for I know that ye seek Jesus, which was crucified. He is not here: for he is risen, as he said. Come, see the place where the Lord lay.'' Matthew 28:5, 6.

Question: **The angel quoted Jesus, using the words, "as he said." What exactly had Jesus said about His resurrection? John, can you tell us?**

Answer: "Therefore doth my Father love me, because I lay down my life, that I might take it again. No man taketh it from me, but I lay it down of myself. I have power to lay it down, and I have power to take it again. This commandment have I received of my Father." John 10:17, 18.

Question: **Now I understand the statement of our Lord, "I am the resurrection." Only God could come up from the tomb by His own power. Paul, were there any witnesses to His resurrection?**

Answer: "He was seen of Cephas, then of the twelve: after that, he was seen of above five hundred brethren at once; of whom the greater part remain unto this present, but some are fallen asleep. After that, he was seen of James; then of all the apostles." 1 Corinthians 15:5-7.

Question: **John, will you describe the touching scene when Thomas finally believed?**

Answer: "Then saith he to Thomas, Reach hither thy finger, and behold my hands; and reach hither thy hand, and thrust it into my side: and be not faithless, but believing. And Thomas answered and said unto him, My Lord and my God." John 20:27, 28.

Thank you, gentlemen of the panel, for your participation. You have established beyond reasonable doubt that Jesus Christ is God. May those who read this record understand and believe to the saving of the soul. The coming of Christ to this earth was the supreme moment of history. By His cross men will be tested, by His love enfolded, and by His grace redeemed. That all who read this record may have this blessed experience is the author's prayer. Amen.

J. BYRON LOGAN

Seeing life under the microscope convinces some scientists that the Creator of life is not some impersonal force, but that He that planted the ear can hear, He that formed the eye can see. See Psalm 94:9.

Creation or Evolution?

2

Creation or Evolution?

Nothing intrigues the mind of man more than the origin of the universe. Science continues to probe nature's storehouse for her secrets. It is seeking a key to the past for the benefit of the present and the future. In this area science is severely handicapped, for it has based its conclusions on the faulty premise that present complicated forms of life evolved from less complicated forms. By this theory nature becomes her own mother, which in itself is contrary to reason.

The evolutionist attributes everything to natural law but becomes exceedingly vague when confronted with the fact that someone must have made the law that governs nature. Law has not been scientifically proved to be self-generative.

When his arguments are not convincing, the evolutionist resorts to ridicule. Reflections on the intelligence of the skeptical hammer many into line. As a matter of fact, evolution is the most unscientific of theories. Its denial of a Creator, God, is its most damaging weakness. It will continue to appeal to true reason in vain until it acknowledges this. By every known law of logic there can be no law, natural or otherwise, without an intelligent lawgiver. Chance and accident could not possibly produce the natural marvels that greet our eyes. It would be like asserting that the automobile or the airplane just happened without any inventor or manufacturer.

And who can say that much of the delinquency and moral irresponsibility that plague our world may not, indeed, be traced to man's low estimate of his own origin—that man is a product of his environment and essentially animal in nature. We turn to the prophets, for God has revealed to them the origin of the universe and the destiny of our world.

Question: **Moses, is it a fact, as some claim, that the world in which we live is a product of the sun?**

Answer: "In the beginning God created the heaven and the earth." Genesis 1:1.

Question: **David, how did He do it?**

Answer: "By the word of the Lord were the heavens made; and all the host of them by the breath of his mouth. . . . For he spake, and it was done; he commanded, and it stood fast." Psalm 33:6-9.

Question: **Moses, how long did it take God to make this planet?**

Answer: "In six days the Lord made heaven and earth, the sea, and all that in them is, and rested the seventh day: wherefore the Lord blessed the sabbath day, and hallowed it." Exodus 20:11.

Question: **How long was each day of Creation?**

Answer: "And God called the light Day, and the darkness he called Night. And the evening and the morning were the first day." Genesis 1:5.

Question: **If we can discover when the evening begins, we will know the length of the day. Mark, when does the evening begin?**

Answer: "At even, when the sun did set, they brought unto him all that were diseased, and them that were possessed with devils." Mark 1:32.

Question: **Moses, what marks off an ordinary day of the week?**

Answer: "From even unto even, shall ye celebrate your sabbath." Leviticus 23:32.

Question: **Then the days of Creation were twenty-four-hour days. Thank you. Now, some scientists contend that man came from a one-celled amoeba. Isaiah, what did you hear God say?**

Answer: "I have made the earth, and created man upon it: I, even my hands, have stretched out the heavens, and all their host have I commanded." Isaiah 45:12.

Question: **Moses, tell us how God created the first man and woman.**

Answer: "The Lord God formed man of the dust of the ground, and breathed into his nostrils the breath of life; and man became a living soul." "The Lord God caused a deep sleep to fall upon Adam, and he slept: and he took one of his ribs, and closed up the flesh instead thereof; and the rib, which the Lord God had taken from man, made he a woman, and brought her unto the man.'' Genesis 2:7, 21, 22.

Question: **That makes sense. God made man and woman on the same day. Did they resemble God in any respect? Moses, you can help us here.**

Answer: ''So God created man in his own image, in the image of God created he him; male and female created he them.'' Genesis 1:27.

Question: **That is understandable. When I consider the many intricate systems that constitute man—nervous, respiratory, alimentary, muscular, and bone—the conclusion is inescapable. Only a supremely intelligent God could have conceived him. The Bible explanation agrees with all laws of logic. Evolutionist, believer in factless theory, great is your faith! Yours is an idol god. Jeremiah, what will become of all who follow false theories?**

Answer: ''The Lord is the true God, he is the living God, and an everlasting king: at his wrath the earth shall tremble, and the nations shall not be able to abide his indignation.'' Jeremiah 10:10.

Question: **While we still have you with us, Jeremiah, please tell us how God conceived and created our universe?**

Answer: ''He hath made the earth by his power, he hath established the world by his wisdom, and hath stretched out the heavens by his discretion.'' Jeremiah 10:12.

Question: **Good! Are there laws that govern the times and seasons of the year, and who made them?**

Answer: ''And God said, Let there be lights in the firmament of the heaven to divide the day from the night; and let them be for signs, and for seasons, and for days, and years.'' Genesis 1:14.

Question: **In spite of some variations, how fixed are the God-given laws of nature as they relate to the seasons?**

Answer: ''While the earth remaineth, seedtime and harvest, and cold and heat, and summer and winter, and day and night shall not cease.'' Genesis 8:22.

Question: **Moses, why don't the mighty seas completely cover** the land? Is there a law, and if so, who made it?

Answer: "Who shut up the sea with doors, whe forth, as if it had issued out of the womb? . . . and erto shalt thou come, but no further: and here shall waves be stayed?" Job 38:8-11.

Question: Are there laws that govern the heavens?

Answer: "Canst thou bind the sweet influences of Pleiades, or loose the bands of Orion? Canst thou bring forth Mazzaroth in his season? or canst thou guide Arcturus with his sons? Knowest thou the ordinances of heaven? canst thou set the dominion thereof in the earth?" Job 38:31-33.

Question: Moses, in the face of God's power so evident in Creation, what confession did Job make that may well be the attitude of all?

Answer: "I know that thou canst do every thing, and that no thought can be withholden from thee. . . . I have heard of thee by the hearing of the ear: but now mine eye seeth thee." Job 42:2-5.

Question: Paul, what have you to say of those who accept debatable theories that rob God of His high place in human esteem?

Answer: "When they knew God, they glorified him not as God, neither were thankful; but became vain in their imaginations, and their foolish heart was darkened. Professing themselves to be wise, they became fools." Romans 1:21, 22.

Question: What effect do theories such as evolution, modernism, and humanism have on behavior?

Answer: They "changed the glory of the uncorruptible God into an image made like to corruptible man, and to birds, and fourfooted beasts, and creeping things. Wherefore God also gave them up to uncleanness through the lusts of their own hearts, to dishonour their own bodies between themselves." Romans 1:23, 24.

Question: What, essentially, is the nature of this intellectual rebellion against God?

Answer: They "changed the truth of God into a lie, and worshipped and served the creature more than the Creator, who is blessed for ever." Romans 1:25.

Thank you, gentlemen. Paul, you have put your finger on the kernel of man's revolt against God; namely, the rejection of

21

anything man cannot fully comprehend intellectually. Thus, man has made the human intellect his final judge or determinant of truth. This is intolerable. The creature is not judge of the Creator. The opposite is true. With our God-given minds we may pursue truth but never doubt its source. We may discover truth but claim no credit for its existence. God often permits man revealing glimpses of His secrets, not to lead him into the strange bypaths of atheism or the slime pit of evolutionary speculation, but to strengthen faith in the Source of all wisdom. What gems of truth still elude us because God cannot trust us with His secrets! With the little he knows, man becomes a "presumptuous pygmy," swollen with unbelief. He so easily forgets that "he is a mere spider, spinning webs in the basement of the universe."

Then let us remember that it is He who has made us and not we ourselves. With this faith let us pursue the Creator with the passion of the hart for the waterbrook or the bee searching for the flower's nectar. Let us worship Him in truth who made heaven and earth, the seas, and the fountains of waters. Let us return to a loving God the love that He has so freely and graciously bestowed on us.

The vastness of the ocean and its ceaseless motion eclipse man's puny power and remind us of the Creator, who formed the earth to be an abode for man, and over which he was to rule.

PAINTING BY DAVID JAMES

The New Birth

3

The New Birth

What must I do to be saved? This is the most serious question a person will ever face. It is the life-and-death question of all the ages. It is a question with an answer, a God-given answer. Only the prophets can help us here. To them we turn for answers.

Question: **Paul, how is a sinner regarded—in a spiritual sense?**
Answer: "You, being dead in your sins and the uncircumcision of your flesh, hath he quickened together with him, having forgiven you all trespasses." Colossians 2:13.

Question: **Paul, will you further describe the living dead?**
Answer: "She that liveth in pleasure is dead while she liveth." 1 Timothy 5:6.

Question: **Sin is a triple poison. It causes spiritual death, physical death, and death in hell-fire. Is that correct? What about physical death, James?**
Answer: "Then when lust hath conceived, it bringeth forth sin: and sin, when it is finished, bringeth forth death." James 1:15.

Question: **David, what about hell-fire?**
Answer: "The wicked shall be turned into hell, and all the nations that forget God." Psalm 9:17.

Question: **Paul, what evidence do we have that the sin in Eden caused man to die spiritually?**
Answer: "All have sinned, and come short of the glory of God." Romans 3:23.

Question: **Moses, what has this to do with Adam and Eve?**

Answer: "The eyes of them both were opened, and they knew that they were naked; and they sewed fig leaves together, and made themselves aprons." Genesis 3:7.

Question: **Only after they sinned were they aware of being naked. They were short of the glory of God. John, how would you describe the lukewarm members of the church today?**
Answer: "Thou sayest, I am rich, and increased with goods, and have need of nothing; and knowest not that thou art wretched, and miserable, and poor, and blind, and naked." Revelation 3:17.

Question: **How did the sin of Adam affect the whole human family? Paul, will you help us?**
Answer: "As by one man sin entered into the world, and death by sin; . . . death passed upon all men, for that all have sinned." Romans 5:12.

Question: **David, how would you describe man's natural depravity?**
Answer: "Behold, I was shapen in iniquity; and in sin did my mother conceive me." Psalm 51:5.

Question: **Paul, will you add one final word to this?**
Answer: "I know that in me (that is, in my flesh,) dwelleth no good thing: for to will is present with me; but how to perform that which is good I find not." Romans 7:18.

Question: **What does this natural, sinful condition of man lead him to do?**
Answer: "The works of the flesh are manifest, which are these; Adultery, fornication, uncleanness, lasciviousness, idolatry, witchcraft, hatred, variance, emulations, wrath, strife, seditions, heresies, envyings, murders, drunkenness, revellings, and such like: of the which I tell you before, as I have also told you in time past, that they which do such things shall not inherit the kingdom of God." Galatians 5:19-21.

Question: **What, John, did Jesus say is a real necessity for every man and woman?**
Answer: "Marvel not that I said unto thee, Ye must be born again." John 3:7.

Question: **Thus, only through the new birth may we regain the spiritual nature that Adam lost. John, what reason did Jesus give for insisting on this experience?**

PAINTING BY HARRY ANDERSON · © BY REVIEW AND HERALD

Christ and Nicodemus, a well-educated Jewish leader, discuss the important question of how a sinner can escape from himself and become a new man—born again "of water and of the Spirit."

Answer: "Jesus answered and said unto him, Verily, verily, I say unto thee, Except a man be born again, he cannot see the kingdom of God." John 3:3.

Question: **That is clear. Only those born again can understand the privileges and disciplines of citizenship in the kingdom of God on earth and in heaven. Did Jesus add to this, John?**

Answer: "Jesus answered, Verily, verily, I say unto thee, Except a man be born of water and of the Spirit, he cannot enter into the kingdom of God." John 3:5.

Question: **Emphatic, concise, understandable. Who is the author of the new birth?**

Answer: "And being made perfect, he became the author of eternal salvation unto all them that obey him." Hebrews 5:9.

Question: **By what act did He initiate the new birth?**

Answer: "But God commendeth his love toward us, in that, while we were yet sinners, Christ died for us." Romans 5:8.

Question: **In what sense may His death affect all sinners?**

Answer: "God so loved the world, that he gave his only begotten Son, that whosoever believeth in him should not perish, but have everlasting life." John 3:16.

Question: **With what touching words, Matthew, did Christ invite the sinner to partake of His generous offer of salvation?**

Answer: "Come unto me, all ye that labour and are heavy laden, and I will give you rest. Take my yoke upon you, and learn of me; for I am meek and lowly in heart: and ye shall find rest unto your souls." Matthew 11:28, 29.

Question: **What is required of the sinner at this point, Isaiah?**

Answer: "If ye be willing and obedient, ye shall eat the good of the land: but if ye refuse and rebel, ye shall be devoured with the sword: for the mouth of the Lord hath spoken it." Isaiah 1:19, 20.

Question: **That's reasonable enough. There must be cooperation, based on willingness to be saved. God will not drag a resisting sinner into His kingdom. Paul, with what power does God convert the willing heart to Christ?**

Answer: "The love of Christ constraineth us; because we thus judge, that if one died for all, then were all dead." 2 Corinthians 5:14.

Question: **Paul, how is this love administered to men?**

Answer: "Hope maketh not ashamed; because the love of God is shed abroad in our hearts by the Holy Ghost which is given unto us." Romans 5:5.

Question: **Thank you, Paul. What infallible proof have we that Christ really loves us?**

Answer: "When we were yet without strength, in due time Christ died for the ungodly." Romans 5:6.

Question: **What should be our initial response to this act of love?**

Answer: "Without faith it is impossible to please him: for he that cometh to God must believe that he is, and that he is a rewarder of them that diligently seek him." Hebrews 11:6.

Question: **God's love for man builds man's faith in God. But where does faith originate? Paul, can you help us?**

Answer: "By grace are ye saved through faith; and that not of yourselves: it is the gift of God." Ephesians 2:8.

Question: **Upon whom has the priceless gift of faith been bestowed, Paul?**

Answer: "For I say, through the grace given unto me, to every man that is among you, not to think of himself more highly than he ought to think; but to think soberly, according as God hath dealt to every man the measure of faith." Romans 12:3.

Question: **How can a man build on his God-given faith and increase it?**

Answer: "So then faith cometh by hearing, and hearing by the word of God." Romans 10:17.

Question: **What further response does the love of God inspire in the heart of the earnest seeker? Luke, can you answer?**

Answer: "Repent ye therefore, and be converted, that your sins may be blotted out, when the times of refreshing shall come from the presence of the Lord." Acts 3:19.

Question: **What act of God produces this attitude in man's heart?**

Answer: "Despisest thou the riches of his goodness and forbearance and longsuffering; not knowing that the goodness of God leadeth thee to repentance?'' Romans 2:4.

Question: **Isaiah, what does repentance mean?**

Answer: ''Seek ye the Lord while he may be found, call ye upon him while he is near: let the wicked forsake his way, and the unrighteous man his thoughts: and let him return unto the Lord, and he will have mercy upon him; and to our God, for he will abundantly pardon.'' Isaiah 55:6, 7.

Question: **When the sinner reaches this point, what comforting thought sustains him? David, help us.**

Answer: ''The Lord is nigh unto them that are of a broken heart; and saveth such as be of a contrite spirit.'' Psalm 34:18.

Question: **Ezekiel, how does God answer the prayer of the contrite?**

Answer: ''I will give them one heart, and I will put a new spirit within you; and I will take the stony heart out of their flesh, and will give them a heart of flesh.'' Ezekiel 11:19.

Question: **Thank you, Ezekiel. What does this enable the sinner to do by God's grace?**

Answer: ''That they may walk in my statutes, and keep mine ordinances, and do them: and they shall be my people, and I will be their God.'' Ezekiel 11:20.

Question: **David, please repeat for us your own prayer of repentant faith.**

Answer: ''Purge me with hyssop, and I shall be clean: wash me, and I shall be whiter than snow. Make me to hear joy and gladness; that the bones which thou hast broken may rejoice. Hide thy face from my sins, and blot out all mine iniquities. Create in me a clean heart, O God; and renew a right spirit within me.'' Psalm 51:7-10.

Question: **Thank you, David. Paul, describe for us the experience of conversion.**

Answer: ''Be not conformed to this world: but be ye transformed by the renewing of your mind, that ye may prove what is that good, and acceptable, and perfect, will of God.'' Romans 12:2.

Question: **How often should this renewal take place?**

Answer: ''For which cause we faint not; but though our outward man perish, yet the inward man is renewed day by day." 2 Corinthians 4:16.

Question: **How deep must this experience be, Paul?**

Answer: "Be renewed in the spirit of your mind; and that ye put on the new man, which after God is created in righteousness and true holiness." Ephesians 4:23, 24.

Question: **Paul, what effect will this have on our behavior?**

Answer: "Let him that stole steal no more. . . . Let no corrupt communication proceed out of your mouth. . . . Grieve not the holy Spirit of God. . . . Let all bitterness, and wrath, and anger, and clamour, and evil speaking, be put away from you, with all malice." Ephesians 4:28-31.

Question: **So true transformation reforms the habits and disciplines the life. At the point of conversion a man is truly born of the Spirit. He becomes a blood-washed son of God. What is the first commandment he must obey after conversion? Luke, will you answer?**

Answer: "Then Peter said unto them, Repent, and be baptized every one of you in the name of Jesus Christ for the remission of sins, and ye shall receive the gift of the Holy Ghost." Acts 2:38.

Question: **Why will we need the Holy Spirit after baptism?**

Answer: "Howbeit when he, the Spirit of truth, is come, he will guide you into all truth: for he shall not speak of himself; but whatsoever he shall hear, that shall he speak: and he will shew you things to come." John 16:13.

Question: **Thereafter, through the Spirit, what additional blessing is ours, John?**

Answer: "He shall glorify me: for he shall receive of mine, and shall shew it unto you." John 16:14.

Question: **Through the Spirit, how does Christ become a living reality in us?**

Answer: "For it is God which worketh in you both to will and to do of his good pleasure." Philippians 2:13.

Question: **With this blessing, what testimony can the Christian make?**

Answer: "I can do all things through Christ which strengtheneth me." Philippians 4:13.

Question: **John, what did Jesus say of the program of the Christian after baptism?**

Answer: "If ye love me, keep my commandments." John 14:15.

Question: **What is the secret of our obedience?**

Answer: "What the law could not do, in that it was weak through the flesh, God sending his own Son in the likeness of sinful flesh, and for sin, condemned sin in the flesh: that the righteousness of the law might be fulfilled in us; who walk not after the flesh, but after the Spirit." Romans 8:3, 4.

Question: **So God's law becomes a way of life, operating as a principle in our lives. Good. Now, in what sense is a converted man free from the law, Paul?**

Answer: "There is therefore now no condemnation to them which are in Christ Jesus, who walk not after the flesh, but after the Spirit." Romans 8:1.

Question: **Then we are free from the law's condemnation when we are led by the Spirit to obey it. Good. Isn't this exactly what God promised?**

Answer: "This is the covenant that I will make with the house of Israel after those days, saith the Lord; I will put my laws into their mind, and write them in their hearts: and I will be to them a God, and they shall be to me a people." Hebrews 8:10.

Question: **How long is God able to preserve in us this "saved" experience?**

Answer: "Being confident of this very thing, that he which hath begun a good work in you will perform it until the day of Jesus Christ." Philippians 1:6.

Question: **This promise is conditional. Do you agree, Ezekiel?**

Answer: "But when the righteous turneth away from his righteousness, and committeth iniquity, and doeth according to all the abominations that the wicked man doeth, shall he live? All his righteousness that he hath done shall not be mentioned: in his trespass that he hath trespassed, and in his sin that he hath sinned, in them shall he die." Ezekiel 18:24.

Question: **The Christian must remain in a state of willingness for God to keep him, or he will lose his way. If this happens, is there any hope?**

Answer: "Again, when the wicked man turneth away from his wickedness that he hath committed, and doeth that which is lawful and right, he shall save his soul alive." Ezekiel 18:27.

Question: **On whom must the Christian rely for his continued salvation?**

Answer: "Him that is able to keep you from falling, and to present you faultless before the presence of his glory with exceeding joy." Jude 24.

Question: **Though temptations assail us with the strength of a gale, of what may we be confident?**

Answer: "God is our refuge and strength, a very present help in trouble." Psalm 46:1.

Question: **Isaiah, give us a parting word.**

Answer: "Thou wilt keep him in perfect peace, whose mind is stayed on thee: because he trusteth in thee. Trust ye in the Lord for ever: for in the Lord Jehovah is everlasting strength." Isaiah 26:3, 4.

Can a Man
Be Perfect?

4

Can a Man Be Perfect?

God has stated the plan of salvation in such terms that the most humble can grasp it by faith. But the simplicity of the gospel has suffered much from theological debate and expert analysis. Were the obscure and devious reasoning of the theologian scrapped and the simple statements of Christ and the prophets taken at their face value, the honest seeker for truth would in them find light and life. To them we turn in this discussion for the wisdom of the ages, for they speak to our day as truly as they did to their own.

Question: **I believe, Matthew, that the angel has an opening statement for us, does he not?**
Answer: "She [Mary] shall bring forth a son, and thou shalt call his name Jesus: for he shall save his people from their sins." Matthew 1:21.

Question: **Luke, who was this angel?**
Answer: "And in the sixth month the angel Gabriel was sent from God unto a city of Galilee, named Nazareth." Luke 1:26.

Question: **How did he address the virgin Mary?**
Answer: "The angel came in unto her, and said, Hail, thou that art highly favoured, the Lord is with thee: blessed art thou among women." Luke 1:28.

Question: **Luke, what was the true identity of the child being born to her?**
Answer: "The angel answered and said unto her, The Holy Ghost shall come upon thee, and the power of the Highest shall overshadow thee: therefore also that holy thing which shall be born of thee shall be called the Son of God." Luke 1:35.

Question: **How did the angel describe the birth of our Saviour?**

Answer: "The angel said unto them, Fear not: for, behold, I bring you good tidings of great joy, which shall be to all people." Luke 2:10.

Question: **Why is this birth so important to all people?**

Answer: "For unto you is born this day in the city of David a Saviour, which is Christ the Lord." Luke 2:11.

Question: **Paul, how does Christ save men?**

Answer: "By grace are ye saved through faith; and that not of yourselves: it is the gift of God." Ephesians 2:8.

Question: **So we are saved by God's unmerited favor and love toward us. Good! But only through God-given faith. Paul, do all men have some faith?**

Answer: "I say, through the grace given unto me, to every man that is among you, not to think of himself more highly than he ought to think; but to think soberly, according as God hath dealt to every man the measure of faith." Romans 12:3.

Question: **So by the exercise of our God-given faith in Christ, we are saved from sin. Is this correct?**

Answer: "Believe on the Lord Jesus Christ, and thou shalt be saved, and thy house." Acts 16:31.

Question: **John, in what words does Jesus confirm this?**

Answer: "For God so loved the world, that he gave his only begotten Son, that whosoever believeth in him should not perish, but have everlasting life." John 3:16.

Question: **What did Christ say then?**

Answer: "God sent not his Son into the world to condemn the world; but that the world through him might be saved." John 3:17.

Question: **What alone will condemn the world, John?**

Answer: "This is the condemnation, that light is come into the world, and men loved darkness rather than light, because their deeds were evil." John 3:19.

Question: **Suppose I am religious but do not accept Christ as my Saviour. Can I be saved?**

Answer: "A man is not justified by the works of the law, but by the faith of Jesus Christ, even we have believed in Jesus

Christ, that we might be justified by the faith of Christ, and not by the works of the law: for by the works of the law shall no flesh be justified.'' Galatians 2:16.

Question: **It is clear that we are not saved by faithless works. But what about workless faith, James?**

Answer: ''Even so faith, if it hath not works, is dead, being alone.'' James 2:17.

Question: **Are you saying, James, that living faith is** *active?*

Answer: ''Yea, a man may say, Thou hast faith, and I have works: shew me thy faith without thy works, and I will shew thee my faith by my works.'' James 2:18.

Question: **Obedience, then, is an outgrowth of living faith. It is a manifestation of the nature of faith. If faith is alive, it works. May we conclude, then, that we are saved by living faith in Christ** *alone?* **And does it work? James, will you answer?**

Answer: ''Thou believest that there is one God; thou doest well: the devils also believe, and tremble. But wilt thou know, O vain man, that faith without works is dead? . . . Seest thou how faith wrought with his works, and by works was faith made perfect?'' James 2:19-22.

Question: **What about the nature of grace? We know what it does for man, but does grace do anything** *to* **the man? Paul, will you help us on this?**

Answer: ''The grace of God that bringeth salvation hath appeared to all men, teaching us that, denying ungodliness and worldly lusts, we should live soberly, righteously, and godly, in this present world.'' Titus 2:11, 12.

Question: **Would you say then, Paul, that grace enforces the law of God in the life of the believer? It is the law that defines sobriety, righteousness, and godliness.**

Answer: ''What the law could not do, in that it was weak through the flesh, God sending his own Son in the likeness of sinful flesh, and for sin, condemned sin in the flesh: that the righteousness of the law might be fulfilled in us, who walk not after the flesh, but after the Spirit.'' Romans 8:3, 4.

Question: **It is the flesh that the law condemns, and when by faith in Christ we receive the new nature the law no longer condemns us, for our lives are shaped by grace through faith into** harmony with the divine law. Good. What is the nature of God's love? Does it affect man?

Answer: "The love of Christ constraineth us; because we thus judge, that if one died for all, then were all dead." 2 Corinthians 5:14.

Question: **Exactly what does God's love accomplish in us? Paul, will you answer?**

Answer: "Be not conformed to this world: but be ye transformed by the renewing of your mind, that ye may prove what is that good, and acceptable, and perfect, will of God." Romans 12:2.

Question: **It is the love of God that transforms the life and renews the mind daily. What is required of those who love God? John, what did Jesus say about that?**

Answer: "If ye love me, keep my commandments." John 14:15.

Question: **It is thus that love is the fulfilling of the law. Thank you, John. Paul, will people who have truly been "saved" be obedient?**

Answer: "And being made perfect, he became the author of eternal salvation unto all them that obey him." Hebrews 5:9.

Question: **Paul, are those who do what the law requires justified?**

Answer: "Not the hearers of the law are just before God, but the doers of the law shall be justified." Romans 2:13.

Question: **Moses, when man sinned, did he seek God or did God seek him? Who initiated the plan of salvation?**

Answer: "They heard the voice of the Lord God walking in the garden in the cool of the day: and Adam and his wife hid themselves from the presence of the Lord God amongst the trees of the garden." Genesis 3:8.

Question: **Salvation, then, is God seeking lost man, out of a heart of love. Paul, would you agree?**

Answer: "God was in Christ, reconciling the world unto himself, not imputing their trespasses unto them; and hath committed unto us the word of reconciliation." 2 Corinthians 5:19.

Question: **At Calvary as in Eden, do we not find God seeking man again?**

Answer: "When we were yet without strength, in due time Christ died for the ungodly." Romans 5:6.

Question: **Christ's death saved us from sin, by faith in this act. Those who lived before the cross demonstrated their faith in the Sacrifice to come by offering sacrifices under the Levitical ritual. Those of us after the cross express our faith in the death of Christ at the communion supper. Before and after the cross, therefore, men are saved by grace through faith. Paul, the Bible says that we are saved from sin by grace. Does this mean that we don't have to obey God's law?**

Answer: "What shall we say then? Is the law sin? God forbid. Nay, I had not known sin, but by the law: for I had not known lust, except the law had said, Thou shalt not covet." Romans 7:7.

Question: **God's saving grace delivers us from the law's condemnation, but not from its jurisdiction. Who, under grace, enforces God's law in the Christian life, Paul?**

Answer: "This is the covenant that I will make with the house of Israel after those days, saith the Lord; I will put my laws into their mind, and write them in their hearts: and I will be to them a God, and they shall be to me a people." Hebrews 8:10.

Question: **Paul, what does God expect of us in view of His matchless love?**

Answer: "We pray always for you, that our God would count you worthy of this calling, and fulfil all the good pleasure of his goodness, and the work of faith with power." 2 Thessalonians 1:11.

Question: **Active faith is the prime essential. That is clear. We also know that God adds to our faith when we read His Word (Romans 10:17) and when we pray (Matthew 7:7), exercising the faith that we have. When we believe in Christ, what will this do to our attitude, Paul?**

Answer: "Despisest thou the riches of his goodness and forbearance and longsuffering; not knowing that the goodness of God leadeth thee to repentance?" Romans 2:4.

Question: **What does repentance include, James?**

Answer: "Submit yourselves therefore to God. Resist the devil, and he will flee from you." James 4:7.

Question: **John, have you anything to add?**

Answer: "If we confess our sins, he is faithful and just to forgive us our sins, and to cleanse us from all unrighteousness." 1 John 1:9.

Question: **Along with this there occurs, in man, a process known as conversion. Describe this experience for us, Paul.**

Answer: You "have put on the new man, which is renewed in knowledge after the image of him that created him." Colossians 3:10.

Question: **David, recite your prayer that brought converting power into your soul.**

Answer: "Create in me a clean heart, O God; and renew a right spirit within me. . . . Restore unto me the joy of thy salvation; and uphold me with thy free spirit." Psalm 51:10-12.

Question: **At this point a man is saved from sin by grace, through faith in the Lord Jesus Christ. What is the first command that a saved man obeys after conversion?**

Answer: "Then Peter said unto them, Repent, and be baptized every one of you in the name of Jesus Christ for the remission of sins, and ye shall receive the gift of the Holy Ghost." Acts 2:38.

Question: **After baptism, what other commandments will a saved man keep?**

Answer: "Whoso looketh into the perfect law of liberty, and continueth therein, he being not a forgetful hearer, but a doer of the work, this man shall be blessed in his deed." James 1:25.

Question: **James, you speak of a law of liberty. Can you further identify this law for us? Give us a few excerpts from it.**

Answer: "He that said, Do not commit adultery, said also, do not kill. Now if thou commit no adultery, yet if thou kill, thou art become a transgressor of the law. So speak ye, and so do, as they that shall be judged by the law of liberty." James 2:11, 12.

Question: **Thank you, James. That is clear. I understand, also, that a Christian's obedience is based on belief in, and love and respect for, God. John, have you a final word to add?**

Answer: "Fear none of those things which thou shalt suffer: behold, the devil shall cast some of you into prison, that ye may be tried; and ye shall have tribulation ten days: be thou faithful unto death, and I will give thee a crown of life.'' Revelation 2:10.

Thank you, gentlemen. Now I understand why Paul speaks of salvation as a secret made known through the living witness of Christ. Only the earnest seeker can grasp it. All such embrace the promises of God by faith, and find them to be a *living reality.* "Come ye to the waters" is the Master's invitation. Thousands living and dead have found satisfaction at the fountain of living waters. Men have tried everything else and found only faint flickers of fleeting fancy. "They have tasted the apples of Sodom and found them ashes." "Ho, every one that thirsteth, come ye to the waters, and he that hath no money; come ye, buy, and eat; yea, come, buy wine and milk without money and without price." Isaiah 55:1. Thank you, Isaiah!

Prayer Power

J. BYRON LOGAN

"More things are wrought by prayer than this world dreams of."—Alfred, Lord Tennyson

5

Prayer Power

By telephone man is able to communicate with any point on the globe. By radio men talked between the earth and the moon. Interplanetary conversation, however, is nothing new. For years men have sent messages to, and received them from, a point farther than the sun. Not through man-made media, which often fail, but through the divine art of prayer. The prophets have given much scientific data on this ancient means of interplanetary contact. This interview is likely to be most enlightening.

Question: **David, what assurance have we that earth creatures will find God responsive to their prayers?**
Answer: "The Lord is nigh unto all them that call upon him, to all that call upon him in truth. He will fulfil the desire of them that fear him: he also will hear their cry, and will save them." Psalm 145:18, 19.

Question: **You encourage me, David. But tell me, when is the best time to pray?**
Answer: "Evening, and morning, and at noon, will I pray, and cry aloud: and he shall hear my voice." Psalm 55:17.

Question: **Paul, do you agree?**
Answer: "Pray without ceasing." 1 Thessalonians 5:17.

Question: **Luke, what does Jesus say?**
Answer: "He spake a parable unto them to this end, that men ought always to pray, and not to faint." Luke 18:1.

Question: **That settles it. Whatever we do, we should sanctify it with prayer. We should pray as we breathe. We should live in an attitude of prayer. Good. Now, suppose I don't know how to pray?**

Answer: "Likewise the Spirit also helpeth our infirmities: for we know not what we should pray for as we ought: but the Spirit itself maketh intercession for us with groanings which cannot be uttered." Romans 8:26.

Question: **Talk to God, and He will help you. Thank you, Paul. Once the disciples asked the Lord for help in this. What did He tell them, Luke?**

Answer: "He said unto them, When ye pray, say, Our Father which art in heaven, Hallowed be thy name. Thy kingdom come. Thy will be done, as in heaven, so in earth. Give us day by day our daily bread. And forgive us our sins; for we also forgive every one that is indebted to us. And lead us not into temptation; but deliver us from evil." Luke 11:2-4.

Question: **What caution should we observe with reference to our prayers?**

Answer: "Be not rash with thy mouth, and let not thine heart be hasty to utter any thing before God: for God is in heaven, and thou upon earth: therefore let thy words be few." Ecclesiastes 5:2.

Question: **Some people make all kinds of promises to God on their knees. Isn't this dangerous?**

Answer: "Better is it that thou shouldest not vow, than that thou shouldest vow and not pay. Suffer not thy mouth to cause thy flesh to sin; neither say thou before the angel, that it was an error: wherefore should God be angry at thy voice, and destroy the work of thine hands?" Ecclesiastes 5:5, 6.

Question: **What are some of the things that we should say when we pray?**

Answer: "Say ye, Save us, O God of our salvation, and gather us together, and deliver us from the heathen, that we may give thanks to thy holy name, and glory in thy praise." 1 Chronicles 16:35.

Question: **How does God regard a praying man?**

Answer: "He shall pray unto God, and he will be favourable unto him: and he shall see his face with joy: for he will render unto men his righteousness." Job 33:26.

Question: **Should we not also remember the work of God in the earth?**

Answer: "Pray ye therefore the Lord of the harvest, that he will send forth labourers into his harvest." Matthew 9:38.

Question: **Mark, what is one absolute essential to answered prayer? What did Jesus say?**

Answer: "Therefore I say unto you, What things soever ye desire, when ye pray, believe that ye receive them, and ye shall have them." Mark 11:24.

Question: **And what if you have a grudge against any?**

Answer: "When ye stand praying, forgive, if ye have ought against any: that your Father also which is in heaven may forgive you your trespasses." Mark 11:25.

Question: **What wise counsel did Jesus give with reference to temptation, Luke?**

Answer: "When he was at the place, he said unto them, Pray that ye enter not into temptation." Luke 22:40.

Question: **Mark, how does Jesus rate the strength of prayer with that of demons?**

Answer: "He said unto them, This kind can come forth by nothing, but by prayer and fasting." Mark 9:29.

Question: **Would you say that prayer is helpful in severe illness, James?**

Answer: "Is any sick among you? let him call for the elders of the church; and let them pray over him, anointing him with oil in the name of the Lord: and the prayer of faith shall save the sick, and the Lord shall raise him up; and if he have committed sins, they shall be forgiven him. Confess your faults one to another, and pray one for another, that ye may be healed. The effectual fervent prayer of a righteous man availeth much." James 5:14-16.

Question: **How can I strengthen my faith so that my prayers may be heard?**

Answer: "Faith cometh by hearing, and hearing by the word of God." Romans 10:17.

Question: **What two things must we believe as we approach the throne of God?**

Answer: "Without faith it is impossible to please him: for he that cometh to God must believe that he is, and that he is a rewarder of them that diligently seek him." Hebrews 11:6.

Ask the Prophets

Question: **Thank you. Solomon, what further condition is laid down for the answer to our prayers?**

Answer: "He that turneth away his ear from hearing the law, even his prayer shall be abomination." Proverbs 28:9.

Question: **David, do you agree with Solomon?**

Answer: "If I regard iniquity in my heart, the Lord will not hear me." Psalm 66:18.

Question: **John, do you also regard obedience as a condition to answered prayer?**

Answer: "And whatsoever we ask, we receive of him, because we keep his commandments, and do those things that are pleasing in his sight." 1 John 3:22.

Question: **Thank you, John. Now in whose name are we to make our requests of God?**

Answer: "Whatsoever ye shall ask in my name, that will I do, that the Father may be glorified in the Son." John 14:13.

Question: **How, then, may we approach God?**

Answer: "Seeing then that we have a great high priest, that is passed into the heavens, Jesus the Son of God, let us hold fast our profession. For we have not an high priest which cannot be touched with the feeling of our infirmities; but was in all points tempted like as we are, yet without sin. Let us therefore come boldly unto the throne of grace, that we may obtain mercy, and find grace to help in time of need." Hebrews 4:14-16.

Question: **James, Elijah was powerful in prayer, was he not?**

Answer: "Elias was a man subject to like passions as we are, and he prayed earnestly that it might not rain: and it rained not on the earth by the space of three years and six months. And he prayed again, and the heaven gave rain, and earth brought forth her fruit." James 5:17, 18.

Question: **What was his secret, James?**

Answer: "Confess your faults one to another, and pray one for another, that ye may be healed. The effectual fervent prayer of a righteous man availeth much." James 5:16.

Question: **Moses, what happened on one occasion when Israel's complaining displeased the Lord?**

Answer: "When the people complained, it displeased the Lord: and the Lord heard it; and his anger was kindled; and the

**Jesus told a story about a proud Pharisee to whose prayer God was deaf,
and a tax collector whose humble petition God heard and answered.**

fire of the Lord burnt among them, and consumed them that were in the uttermost parts of the camp. And the people cried unto Moses; and when Moses prayed unto the Lord, the fire was quenched." Numbers 11:1, 2.

Question: **Luke, Cornelius, an Italian centurion, was a man of prayer. What was his experience?**

Answer: "Cornelius said, Four days ago I was fasting until this hour; and at the ninth hour I prayed in my house, and, behold, a man stood before me in bright clothing, and said, Cornelius, thy prayer is heard, and thine alms are had in remembrance in the sight of God." Acts 10:30, 31.

Question: **What was Peter's reaction to this unusual experience?**

Answer: "Then Peter opened his mouth, and said, Of a truth I perceive that God is no respecter of persons: but in every nation he that feareth him, and worketh righteousness, is accepted with him." Acts 10:34, 35.

Question: **In His humanity, how deeply did Christ agonize in prayer?**

Answer: "He was withdrawn from them about a stone's cast, and kneeled down, and prayed. . . . And being in an agony he prayed more earnestly: and his sweat was as it were great drops of blood falling down to the ground." Luke 22:41-44.

Question: **Such deep earnestness puts us to shame. And our need is so much greater than His. God help us! Paul, what element should characterize all our prayers?**

Answer: "Be careful for nothing; but in every thing by prayer and supplication with thanksgiving let your requests be made known unto God." Philippians 4:6.

Question: **Luke, two men went to the Temple to pray. Tell us of the first one.**

Answer: "The Pharisee stood and prayed thus with himself, God, I thank thee, that I am not as other men are, extortioners, unjust, adulterers, or even as this publican. I fast twice in the week, I give tithes of all that I possess." Luke 18:11, 12.

Question: **What a prayer! I have heard a few like it in my day. What about the other one?**

Answer: "The publican, standing afar off, would not lift up so much as his eyes unto heaven, but smote upon his breast, saying, God be merciful to me a sinner.'' Luke 18:13.

Question: **Tell us, Luke, which prayer was heard in heaven?**
Answer: ''I tell you, this man went down to his house justified rather than the other: for every one that exalteth himself shall be abased; and he that humbleth himself shall be exalted.'' Luke 18:14.

Question: **Beautiful! Luke, how did Christ say that His church should be known?**
Answer: ''It is written, My house is the house of prayer: but ye have made it a den of thieves.'' Luke 19:46.

Question: **Daniel, you were a good man. When you prayed, what did you do, and with what result?**
Answer: ''Whiles I was speaking, and praying, and confessing my sin and the sin of my people Israel, and presenting my supplication before the Lord my God for the holy mountain of my God; yea, whiles I was speaking in prayer, even the man Gabriel, whom I had seen in the vision at the beginning, being caused to fly swiftly, touched me about the time of the evening oblation.'' Daniel 9:20, 21.

Question: **When Jesus was on earth, how did He demonstrate humanity's need for prayer?**
Answer: ''It came to pass in those days, that he went out into a mountain to pray, and continued all night in prayer to God.'' Luke 6:12.

Question: **Though we may pray at any time, in any posture, what is the recommended posture for prayer?**
Answer: ''For this cause I bow my knees unto the Father of our Lord Jesus Christ.'' Ephesians 3:14.

Question: **David, do you agree?**
Answer: ''O come, let us worship and bow down: let us kneel before the Lord our maker.'' Psalm 95:6.

Question: **Solomon, what was your usual posture in prayer?**
Answer: ''When Solomon had made an end of praying all this prayer and supplication unto the Lord, he arose from before the altar of the Lord, from kneeling on his knees with his hands spread up to heaven.'' 1 Kings 8:54.

Question: **Daniel, what was your custom?**

4

Ask the Prophets

Answer: "When Daniel knew that the writing was signed, he went into his house; and his windows being open in his chamber toward Jerusalem, he kneeled upon his knees three times a day, and prayed, and gave thanks before his God, as he did aforetime." Daniel 6:10.

Thank you, gentlemen, for another helpful symposium. Prayer is the breath of the soul. It is little wonder that so many people are spiritually dead. They pray so little. "Much prayer, much power; little prayer, little power; no prayer, no power." Man is dependent by his very nature. As the flower gathers strength from the soil and the sun and refreshment from the dew and rain, so the soul nourished in the soil of prayer is strengthened by the Sun of righteousness and refreshed by the dew of holiness. Sin is to prayer what jamming is to radio transmission. Static makes transmission barely discernible. Sin blocks the path of prayer to the throne of glory.

There is something fascinating about money, even to young children. In the hands of those who learn how to use it wisely, money proves to be a blessing, to their fellow men as well as themselves.

PHOTO BY J. BYRON LOGAN

Green Power

6

Green Power

It is not sinful to be rich. Money can be a blessing to man, the church, and the world. What has the Bible to say about money? As usual we turn to the prophets for the answers.

Question: **Paul, does the Bible call money the root of all evil?**
Answer: "The love of money is the root of all evil: which while some coveted after, they have erred from the faith, and pierced themselves through with many sorrows." 1 Timothy 6:10.

Question: **What, then, is your counsel to us in view of this?**
Answer: "But thou, O man of God, flee these things; and follow after righteousness, godliness, faith, love, patience, meekness." 1 Timothy 6:11.

Question: **So it is not money but the love of money that is the root of all evil. Solomon, how valuable is money in the everyday affairs of man?**
Answer: "A feast is made for laughter, and wine maketh merry: but money answereth all things." Ecclesiastes 10:19.

Question: **Isaiah, repeat your challenge to men for a more wise use of their money.**
Answer: "Wherefore do ye spend money for that which is not bread? and your labour for that which satisfieth not? hearken diligently unto me, and eat ye that which is good, and let your soul delight itself in fatness." Isaiah 55:2.

Question: **In Bible times, what counsel was given the rich about lending to someone in dire straits?**
Answer: "Thou shalt not lend upon usury to thy brother;

52

usury of money, usury of victuals, usury of any thing that is lent upon usury.'' Deuteronomy 23:19.

Question: **He was not to charge interest? Interesting. Luke, what is more important than money?**
Answer: ''Peter said unto him, Thy money perish with thee, because thou hast thought that the gift of God may be purchased with money.'' Acts 8:20.

Question: **Though riches are a blessing, what is of far greater importance?**
Answer: ''A good name is rather to be chosen than great riches, and loving favour rather than silver and gold.'' Proverbs 22:1.

Question: **Solomon, does money bring with it a sense of satisfaction?**
Answer: ''He that loveth silver shall not be satisfied with silver; nor he that loveth abundance with increase: this is also vanity.'' Ecclesiastes 5:10.

Question: **Why is the love of money said to be ''vanity''?**
Answer: ''When goods increase, they are increased that eat them: and what good is there to the owners thereof, saving the beholding of them with their eyes?'' Ecclesiastes 5:11.

Question: **How does abundance affect sleep?**
Answer: ''The sleep of a labouring man is sweet, whether he eat little or much: but the abundance of the rich will not suffer him to sleep.'' Ecclesiastes 5:12.

Question: **Solomon, what is the appropriate attitude toward money?**
Answer: ''Remove far from me vanity and lies: give me neither poverty nor riches; feed me with food convenient for me.'' Proverbs 30:8.

Question: **Why is this best?**
Answer: ''Lest I be full, and deny thee, and say, Who is the Lord? or lest I be poor, and steal, and take the name of my God in vain.'' Proverbs 30:9.

Question: **Job, you were rich. How did you feel about money?**
Answer: ''If I have made gold my hope, or have said to the fine gold, Thou art my confidence; if I rejoiced because my

wealth was great, and because mine hand had gotten much; . . . this also were an iniquity to be punished by the judge: for I shall have denied the God that is above." Job 31:24-28.

Question: **Isaiah, what priceless gift may be had without money?**

Answer: "Ho, every one that thirsteth, come ye to the waters, and he that hath no money; come ye, buy, and eat; yea, come, buy wine and milk without money and without price." Isaiah 55:1.

Question: **Isaiah, what was true of Israel and Adam is true of us. We were sold into sin for nought. How much money do we need for redemption?**

Answer: "Thus saith the Lord, Ye have sold yourselves for nought; and ye shall be redeemed without money." Isaiah 52:3.

Question: **Paul, is so priceless a possession as salvation absolutely free?**

Answer: "The wages of sin is death; but the gift of God is eternal life through Jesus Christ our Lord." Romans 6:23.

Question: **Obviously, a gift must be accepted. What is involved in that acceptance?**

Answer: "Without faith it is impossible to please him: for he that cometh to God must believe that he is, and that he is a rewarder of them that diligently seek him." Hebrews 11:6.

Question: **Luke, what did the apostle Peter say that might be helpful?**

Answer: "Then Peter said unto them, Repent, and be baptized every one of you in the name of Jesus Christ for the remission of sins, and ye shall receive the gift of the Holy Ghost." Acts 2:38.

Question: **Tell us, Ezekiel, when will the futility of riches be fully revealed?**

Answer: "They shall cast their silver in the streets, and their gold shall be removed: their silver and their gold shall not be able to deliver them in the day of the wrath of the Lord: they shall not satisfy their souls, neither fill their bowels: because it is the stumblingblock of their iniquity." Ezekiel 7:19.

Question: **What, then, must be our primary concern now? Matthew, can you help us?**

Answer: "Seek ye first the kingdom of God, and his right-eousness; and all these things shall be added unto you." Matthew 6:33.

Question: **David, do you agree with Matthew? If I serve the Lord, may I expect His support?**

Answer: "I have been young, and now am old; yet have I not seen the righteous forsaken, nor his seed begging bread." Psalm 37:25.

Thank you, gentlemen. More men than we realize have been corrupted by cash. The peril of plenty has claimed thousands. How easy it is to trust in that which has no permanency, and to build on shifting sand. Blessed is that man whose God is the Lord. In him verily is the word fulfilled—his house is built on a rock!

**Modern young people are confronted with problems no previous genera-
tion had to face. Only in Christ can space-age youth find a solution to these
problems, and lasting happiness.**

Space-Age Youth

7

Space-Age Youth

This is the young man's day. The wisest of our elders knew that it would come. It has come with waving slogan and battle cry. It has come! With strident chant and marching feet, the day of youth has come. With calls for change—some good, some evil—it has come. Tired of solutions that don't solve and potions that don't heal, a new man makes the scene—and he is young! Evolution, even if he believed it, could never content him. It is too slow. His is a revolt against the past, good as well as evil. And with what would he fill the newly created vacuum? He is not sure, but he thinks that can wait. The old must go! Of this much he is sure: Under him, the future will be good, bright, and shiny for all. We must act now; we can plan later. Morality? The religion of squares. *Freedom!* is the bright new slogan. Freedom from all Victorian restraints. Life is a "happening." Let it happen.

Thank God this is not universal. Unheard, unseen, and often unknown, are thousands of thoughtful young people to whom the past is not all good or evil, and who though determined to change the evil would die in defense of the good. To them anarchy poses more problems than those they protest. And to fragment society is to dissolve all hope of reconstruction.

The future course of history is the course of youth. Of supreme importance, then, is this growing segment of our society on whose young shoulders hang the heavy burdens of the future. They need the very best in guidance and counsel. Who but the prophets can supply this need? We turn to them.

Question: **Solomon, what do you think is of basic importance to today's youth? What is indispensable to their balanced development?**

58

Answer: "Remember now thy Creator in the days of thy youth, while the evil days come not, nor the years draw nigh, when thou shalt say, I have no pleasure in them." Ecclesiastes 12:1.

Question: **Belief in the Creator is basic! Perhaps this is because a man who knows not his origin cannot know his destiny. But tell us, Solomon, what attitude should youth take toward parents?**

Answer: "A wise son maketh a glad father: but a foolish son is the heaviness of his mother." Proverbs 10:1.

Question: **Why is it important for youth to submit to their parents?**

Answer: "Correction is grievous unto him that forsaketh the way: and he that hateth reproof shall die." Proverbs 15:10.

Question: **Should youth seek the counsel of their elders in vital matters?**

Answer: "Without counsel purposes are disappointed: but in the multitude of counsellors they are established." Proverbs 15:22.

Question: **Solomon, is this true even though a young man thinks he is right?**

Answer: "There is a way that seemeth right unto a man, but the end thereof are the ways of death." Proverbs 16:25.

Question: **But youth are sometimes too proud to submit to their elders. Is there anything good in such pride?**

Answer: "Better it is to be of an humble spirit with the lowly, than to divide the spoil with the proud." Proverbs 16:19.

Question: **But what of youth who have a desire for money to spend, and who drop out of school to get a job?**

Answer: "How much better is it to get wisdom than gold! and to get understanding rather to be chosen than silver!" Proverbs 16:16.

Question: **Many of today's youth are reckless in speech. Have you counsel for them?**

Answer: "He that hath a froward heart findeth no good: and he that hath a perverse tongue falleth into mischief." Proverbs 17:20.

Question: **Some youth are easily influenced by the guidance of** other youth whose judgment is perverted. Have you help for them?

Answer: "Cease, my son, to hear the instruction that causeth to err from the words of knowledge." Proverbs 19:27.

Question: **Solomon, as an expert on youth would you say that there is any danger in picking the wrong associates?**

Answer: "He that walketh with wise men shall be wise: but a companion of fools shall be destroyed." Proverbs 13:20.

Question: **Paul, is there any class of people that youth would do well to avoid?**

Answer: "But now I have written unto you not to keep company, if any man that is called a brother be a fornicator, or covetous, or an idolater, or a railer, or a drunkard, or an extortioner; with such an one no not to eat." 1 Corinthians 5:11.

Question: **Is it reasonable to expect young people to be responsible for their actions?**

Answer: "Let no man despise thy youth; but be thou an example of the believers, in word, in conversation, in charity, in spirit, in faith, in purity." 1 Timothy 4:12.

Question: **Tell us, Paul, is youth a time for free sexual expression, or should the young practice moral discipline?**

Answer: "Flee also youthful lusts: but follow righteousness, faith, charity, peace, with them that call on the Lord out of a pure heart." 2 Timothy 2:22.

Question: **Then would you say that it is foolish to squander one's substance in immoral living, Solomon?**

Answer: "I discerned among the youths, a young man void of understanding, passing through the street near her corner; and he went the way to her house. . . . He goeth after her straightway, as an ox goeth to the slaughter, or as a fool to the correction of the stocks." Proverbs 7:7-22.

Question: **Solomon, have you a warning for youth who are so inclined?**

Answer: "Hearken unto me now therefore, O ye children, and attend to the words of my mouth. Let not thine heart decline to her ways, go not astray in her paths. For she hath cast down many wounded: yea, many strong men have been slain by her." Proverbs 7:24-26.

Question: **Paul, how do you describe a woman who fails to guard her virtue?**

Answer: "For of this sort are they which creep into houses, and lead captive silly women laden with sins, led away with divers lusts." 2 Timothy 3:6.

Question: **So you call them silly. An appropriate description indeed, when you consider what they stand to lose. Many youth are infatuated with the theater, night clubs, and jazz. John, have you any counsel for them?**

Answer: "Love not the world, neither the things that are in the world. If any man love the world, the love of the Father is not in him." 1 John 2:15.

Question: **That is certainly clear. I know of no one who has called the theater, night club, or jazz music God's form of recreation. But what about LSD, marijuana, heroin, tobacco, and other drugs that turn folks on? Have you something on this, Paul?**

Answer: "Wherefore come out from among them, and be ye separate, saith the Lord, and touch not the unclean thing; and I will receive you." 2 Corinthians 6:17.

Question: **But what about wine, whisky, and beer? The TV ads make them so attractive. Solomon, can you help us?**

Answer: "Wine is a mocker, strong drink is raging: and whosoever is deceived thereby is not wise." Proverbs 20:1.

Question: **Is the practice of drinking alcoholic beverages actually harmful?**

Answer: "At the last it biteth like a serpent, and stingeth like an adder." Proverbs 23:32.

Question: **With all these prohibitions, isn't God just keeping some good things from us?**

Answer: "The Lord God is a sun and shield: the Lord will give grace and glory: no good thing will he withhold from them that walk uprightly." Psalm 84:11.

Question: **So God withholds only what is against man's interest. Great is the Lord! Is God really necessary to the welfare of youth, in view of man's advances in science and technology?**

Answer: "In him we live, and move, and have our being; as certain also of your own poets have said, For we are also his offspring." Acts 17:28.

Question: **Thank you, Paul. It is also noteworthy that many of the men who are involved in our present advance in space are ardent believers in God. But what about the contempt for authority so widespread and evident among youth today?**

Answer: "This know also, that in the last days perilous times shall come. For men shall be lovers of their own selves, covetous, boasters, proud, blasphemers, disobedient to parents, unthankful, unholy, without natural affection, trucebreakers, false accusers, incontinent, fierce, despisers of those that are good, traitors, heady, highminded, lovers of pleasure more than lovers of God." 2 Timothy 3:1-4.

Question: **But will this go on forever, Paul?**

Answer: "They shall proceed no further: for their folly shall be manifest unto all men, as their's also was." 2 Timothy 3:9.

Question: **To avoid this fate, what safeguard did Timothy's mother erect around her son?**

Answer: "From a child thou hast known the holy scriptures, which are able to make thee wise unto salvation through faith which is in Christ Jesus." 2 Timothy 3:15.

Question: **When Jesus was on earth did He take an interest in young people?**

Answer: "Then were there brought unto him little children, that he should put his hands on them, and pray: and the disciples rebuked them. But Jesus said, Suffer little children, and forbid them not, to come unto me: for of such is the kingdom of heaven." Matthew 19:13, 14.

Question: **Matthew, did any youth show an interest in Christ?**

Answer: "And, behold, one came and said unto him, Good Master, what good thing shall I do, that I may have eternal life? And he said unto him, Why callest thou me good? there is none good but one, that is, God: but if thou wilt enter into life, keep the commandments. He saith unto him, Which? Jesus said, Thou shalt do no murder, thou shalt not commit adultery, Thou shalt not steal, Thou shalt not bear false witness, Honour thy father and thy mother: and, Thou shalt love thy neighbour as thyself. The young man saith unto him, All these things have I kept from my youth up: what lack I yet? Jesus said unto him, If thou wilt be perfect, go and sell that thou hast, and give to the poor, and thou shalt have treasure in heaven: and come and follow me. But when the young man heard that saying, he went away sorrowful: for he had great possessions.'' Matthew 19:16-21.

Question: **But what if a young man persists in living the wild life? What would you say to him, Solomon?**

Answer: ''Rejoice, O young man, in thy youth; and let thy heart cheer thee in the days of thy youth, and walk in the ways of thine heart, and in the sight of thine eyes: but know thou, that for all these things God will bring thee into judgment.'' Ecclesiastes 11:9.

Thank you, gentlemen. We close another chapter in the story of man. It is the author's prayer that these words of the prophets will give some youthful traveler pause, that above the din of a million beckoning voices his heart will hear one voice, that of the Son of God, and that hearing he will live. There is a saying that whom the gods would destroy they first make mad. Demon-driven men are exhibiting a degree of madness never seen before on this planet. Satan can field a million pied pipers to lead the unsuspecting to their doom, as indeed he has. Humanity, like a whirling dervish, is in her dance of death. To the maddening beat of a thousand drums she dances on, exhausted yet driven by some unseen force, making each movement wilder than the one before. But it will end, suddenly and dramatically it will end—as when the stone cut out of the mountain without hands demolished the image of Nebuchadnezzar's dream. Jesus Christ will smite the earth in judgment, grinding it to powder. And the wind will blow it away like chaff from the threshing floor. And the stone shall become a great mountain and fill the whole earth.

Thus the kingdoms of this world will become the kingdom of our Lord and of His Christ, and He shall reign forever and ever. ''He shall feed his flock like a shepherd: he shall gather the lambs with his arm, and carry them in his bosom.'' Isaiah 40:11.

Never since the dawn of recorded history has the basic unit of society—the home—been under fiercer assaults than in this present generation.

The Home
Under Assault

8

The Home Under Assault

The home is the smallest unit of organized society. It must survive if civilization is to survive. But there are storm signals ahead. The sanctity of marriage is under brutal attack. Immorality in all of its forms is becoming the common practice. Divorce is becoming respectable and adultery has lost its power to shock. Ours is a sin-conditioned society, and the swift current of the river of iniquity flows downward.

Moreover, basic concepts of decency and morality are being tossed aside as archaic. Virtue is now declared a relic of a bygone age. The decadent are lionized, and the good called square. May we hope for better? Can anything or anyone save us now? For answers we turn to the prophets, for in them verily is the wisdom of God.

Question: **Tell us of the origin of marriage, Moses. How and where did it all begin?**

Answer: "The Lord God caused a deep sleep to fall upon Adam, and he slept: and he took one of his ribs, and closed up the flesh instead thereof; and the rib, which the Lord God had taken from man, made he a woman, and brought her unto the man." Genesis 2:21, 22.

Question: **So God performed the first marriage. He brought Adam and Eve together. Is that still the procedure today in marriage? Matthew, what did Christ say about marriage?**

Answer: "For this cause shall a man leave father and mother, and shall cleave to his wife: and they twain shall be one flesh? Wherefore they are no more twain, but one flesh. What therefore God hath joined together, let not man put asunder." Matthew 19:5, 6.

Question: Paul, what is the only sound basis of a happy marriage?

Answer: "So ought men to love their wives as their own bodies. He that loveth his wife loveth himself." "Wives, submit yourselves unto your own husbands, as unto the Lord. . . . Therefore as the church is subject unto Christ, so let the wives be to their own husbands in every thing." Ephesians 5:28, 22-24.

Question: Moses, may each marriage partner pursue his own separate desires in a sort of unity of diversity?

Answer: "Therefore shall a man leave his father and his mother, and shall cleave unto his wife; and they shall be one flesh." Genesis 2:24.

Question: What law of God was specifically given to safeguard this holy estate? Moses, will you answer?

Answer: "Thou shalt not commit adultery." Exodus 20:14.

Question: This is important. A married man can have only one wife. Is that what you mean, Moses?

Answer: Of "the rib, which the Lord God had taken from man, made he a woman, and brought her unto the man." Genesis 2:22.

Question: So you are saying that God gave Adam one Eve. Good point. Didn't Abraham have two wives? He was a good man.

Answer: "Sarai Abram's wife took Hagar her maid the Egyptian, after Abram had dwelt ten years in the land of Canaan, and gave her to her husband Abram to be his wife. . . . And Sarai said unto Abram, My wrong be upon thee: I have given my maid into thy bosom; and when she saw that she had conceived, I was despised in her eyes: the Lord judge between me and thee." Genesis 16:3, 5.

Question: So there was trouble in Abraham's house because of this violation. Sarah later admitted that in giving her maid to Abraham she did wrong. Malachi, what have you to say about the number of wives a man should have?

Answer: "The Lord hath been witness between thee and the wife of thy youth, against whom thou hast dealt treacherously: yet is she thy companion, and the wife of thy covenant. And did not he make one? Yet had he the residue of the spirit. And wherefore one? That he might seek a godly seed. Therefore take heed to your spirit, and let none deal treacherously against the wife of his youth." Malachi 2:14, 15.

Question: **The act of adultery is condemned in the Scriptures as treachery against one's mate. Solomon, can you cite certain dangers to one guilty of adultery?**

Answer: "By means of a whorish woman a man is brought to a piece of bread: and the adulteress will hunt for the precious life. Can a man take fire in his bosom, and his clothes not be burned? Can one go upon hot coals, and his feet not be burned? So he that goeth in to his neighbour's wife; whosoever toucheth her shall not be innocent. . . . But whoso committeth adultery with a woman lacketh understanding: he that doeth it destroyeth his own soul." Proverbs 6:26-32.

Question: **Thank you, Solomon. But what about the danger of violence? In Proverbs 7:7-21 you speak of a young man whom you correctly describe as simple who commits the adulterous act. How did he die?**

Answer: "With her much fair speech she caused him to yield, with the flattering of her lips she forced him. He goeth after her straightway, as an ox goeth to the slaughter, or as a fool to the correction of the stocks; till a dart strike through his liver; as a bird hasteth to the snare, and knoweth not that it is for his life." Proverbs 7:21-23.

Question: **What about the unmarried? Are they free to engage in sex? Peter, will you answer?**

Answer: "Dearly beloved, I beseech you as strangers and pilgrims, abstain from fleshly lusts, which war against the soul." 1 Peter 2:11.

Question: **Paul, would you be more specific, please.**

Answer: "Flee fornication. . . . He that committeth fornication sinneth against his own body." 1 Corinthians 6:18.

Question: **I understand that the word *fornication* covers all forms of immorality, including sex between unmarried people. Paul, if the unmarried people are not supposed to indulge, why do they have such passionate urges? Is this not the signal to engage in sex?**

Answer: "Now the body is not for fornication, but for the Lord; and the Lord for the body." 1 Corinthians 6:13.

68

Question: So these natural urges do not mean that the unmarried should indulge, but they signify the chemical changes that normally take place as the body prepares itself for the marriage experience. The sex urge in the unmarried then is the good news that they are normal and fitted for marriage and not a signal that wild oats should be sown. Thank you, Paul. What if the urge is overpowering?

Answer: "Let not sin therefore reign in your mortal body, that ye should obey it in the lusts thereof. Neither yield ye your members as instruments of unrighteousness unto sin: but yield yourselves unto God, as those that are alive from the dead, and your members as instruments of righteousness unto God." Romans 6:12, 13.

Question: Thank you, Paul. But how can a man resist the power of human nature? Isaiah, will you answer?

Answer: "Fear thou not; for I am with thee: be not dismayed; for I am thy God: I will strengthen thee; yea, I will help thee; yea, I will uphold thee with the right hand of my righteousness." Isaiah 41:10.

Question: Paul, have you any further suggestion?

Answer: "But now I have written unto you not to keep company, if any man that is called a brother be a fornicator." 1 Corinthians 5:11.

Question: Matthew, how did Jesus describe the moral situation at the end of the world?

Answer: "Because iniquity shall abound, the love of many shall wax cold." Matthew 24:12.

Question: Was Christ more specific, Matthew?

Answer: "As the days of Noe were, so shall also the coming of the Son of man be. For as in the days that were before the flood they were eating and drinking, marrying and giving in marriage, until the day that Noe entered into the ark." Matthew 24:37, 38.

Question: Matthew, didn't Jesus give one basis for divorce and remarriage?

Answer: "I say unto you, Whosoever shall put away his wife, except it be for fornication, and shall marry another, committeth adultery: and whoso marrieth her which is put away doth commit adultery." Matthew 19:9.

Ask the Prophets

Question: **I understand. Christ does not here encourage the offended mate to divorce his wife and remarry. He merely permits it. Paul, what is the rule? How long should the married stay married?**

Answer: "The woman which hath an husband is bound by the law to her husband so long as he liveth; but if the husband be dead, she is loosed from the law of her husband. So then if, while her husband liveth, she be married to another man, she shall be called an adulteress: but if her husband be dead, she is free from that law; so that she is no adulteress, though she be married to another man." Romans 7:2, 3.

Question: **In summary, what do you say of marriage?**

Answer: "Marriage is honourable in all, and the bed undefiled: but whoremongers and adulterers God will judge." Hebrews 13:4.

Thank you, gentlemen. Yours is the only ray of hope in an otherwise dark picture. The morals of youth are being corrupted by the pagan philosophies being urged upon them. Movies, novels, pornographic literature, and personal peddlers of filth take their daily toll. And from many pulpits of the world the moral law of God is denounced as for a bygone age. With this coming from the clergy, small wonder men live without restraint. Fed this continuous stream of satanic venom, the blood stream of human morality has been poisoned. The new generation lives in open sin. Trial marriages, virgin clubs, and sex deviates form the priesthood of the new idolatry. Where will it all end? This world is dancing toward Sodom! Remember history?

The twin cities of the plain, Sodom and Gomorrah, lay shimmering in the pale rays of the setting sun. Her inhabitants were just filling the streets for a night of revelry. These cities had barely one evening to live. As the night wore on, familiar sounds greeted the ear. The heavy beat of the ballroom orchestra hammers the ear as a sea of humanity is caught up in its last dance of death. At the height of the revelry, two strangers slipped quietly into town. These were the angels of judgment. The air was thick with the smell of wine and the curses of the drunken as a mad mob bent on rape groped blindly in search of new victims. Came the gray streak of dawn. A small exodus left unnoticed. Then searing flame and two cities died, suffocated by smoke from Jehovah's furnace. So shall it be in the end of the world.

Angels Are Real

In vision John saw three angels proclaiming God's last message of mercy and warning to the world, and calling upon men to prepare for the soon return of the Lord Jesus Christ in power and glory.

9

Angels Are Real

Some of the most powerful forces in the world are invisible. Be it atom or air, their existence is unquestioned and their power real. That celestial beings are at work on this planet is a fact worthy of our study. In this age of flying saucers and other unidentified objects, the fear has been often expressed that our planet is in danger of invasion by beings from outer space. Many years ago Orson Welles gave such a vivid description of an imaginary war with "other world" soldiers that many people panicked and did unbelievable things.

It may startle you, but the truth is that this world has already been invaded by beings from outer space and conquered. Other beings from outer space are counterattacking with some success. Let us turn to the Bible for a detailed description of these beings and the nature of their work and intervention in the affairs of men.

Question: **David, what is the status of angels as created beings?**
Answer: "What is man, that thou art mindful of him? and the son of man, that thou visitest him? For thou hast made him a little lower than the angels, and hast crowned him with glory and honour." Psalm 8:4, 5.

Question: **The angels, then, are of a higher order of creation than man. Have you any idea of their number?**
Answer: "The chariots of God are twenty thousand, even thousands of angels." Psalm 68:17.

Question: **John, do you agree?**
Answer: "I heard the voice of many angels round about the throne and the beasts and the elders: and the number of them

was ten thousand times ten thousand, and thousands of thousands.'' Revelation 5:11.

Question: **What is said of the vast number of these powerful beings?**

Answer: "But ye are come unto mount Sion, and unto the city of the living God, the heavenly Jerusalem, and to an innumerable company of angels." Hebrews 12:22.

Question: **John, are the angels divine beings and hence to be worshiped?**

Answer: "I fell down to worship before the feet of the angel which shewed me these things. Then saith he unto me, See thou do it not: for I am thy fellowservant, and of thy brethren the prophets, and of them which keep the sayings of this book: worship God." Revelation 22:8, 9.

Question: **Daniel, can you give us a description of an angel?**

Answer: "Then I lifted up mine eyes, and looked, and behold a certain man clothed in linen, whose loins were girded with fine gold of Uphaz: his body also was like the beryl, and his face as the appearance of lightning, and his eyes as lamps of fire, and his arms and his feet like in colour to polished brass, and the voice of his words like the voice of a multitude." Daniel 10:5, 6.

Question: **Moses, how real are the angels?**

Answer: "He took butter, and milk, and the calf which he had dressed, and set it before them; and he stood by them under the tree, and they did eat." Genesis 18:8.

Question: **Then angels are real! Luke, tell us something of their power.**

Answer: "Peter was sleeping between two soldiers, bound with two chains: and the keepers before the door kept the prison. And, behold, the angel of the Lord came upon him, and a light shined in the prison: and he smote Peter on the side; and raised him up, saying, Arise up quickly. And his chains fell off from his hands. And the angel said unto him, Gird thyself, and bind on thy sandals. And so he did. And he saith unto him, Cast thy garment about thee, and follow me." Acts 12:6-8.

Question: **Power? Yes. Luke, I see something else here. This angel was concerned for Peter's health. He took time to remind Peter to take his sandals and a coat. That was thoughtful. But** what of power—angel power? Will you answer, Matthew?

Answer: "Behold, there was a great earthquake: for the angel of the Lord descended from heaven, and came and rolled back the stone from the door, and sat upon it." Matthew 28:2.

Question: That answers my question, and it does more. It tells me that angels are not disembodied spirits! David, do you agree with Matthew about angel power?

Answer: "Bless the Lord, ye his angels, that excel in strength, that do his commandments, hearkening unto the voice of his word." Psalm 103:20.

Question: Again we get more than we requested. Angels are not only powerful, they are obedient to God. They obey His commands. Moses, what important function did the angel perform at the gate of Eden when man was expelled?

Answer: "So he drove out the man; and he placed at the east of the garden of Eden Cherubims, and a flaming sword which turned every way, to keep the way of the tree of life." Genesis 3:24.

Question: Why was that necessary?

Answer: "The Lord God said, Behold the man is become as one of us, to know good and evil: and now, lest he put forth his hand, and take also of the tree of life, and eat, and live for ever: therefore the Lord God sent him forth from the garden of Eden." Genesis 3:22, 23.

Question: Ah! we continue to uncover fresh revelations. We ask for one thing and get much more. Man is not immortal. The angels prevented it. If man had been permitted to eat of the tree, then he would have become an immortal sinner, but God sent His angels to prevent it. Amen! Tell us, Luke, are angels interested in the salvation of sinners?

Answer: "Likewise, I say unto you, there is joy in the presence of the angels of God over one sinner that repenteth." Luke 15:10.

Question: Do all men have access to angel power?

Answer: "Are they not all ministering spirits, sent forth to minister for them who shall be heirs of salvation?" Hebrews 1:14.

Question: Matthew, does that include little children?

Answer: "Take heed that ye despise not one of these little ones; for I say unto you, That in heaven their angels do always behold the face of my Father which is in heaven." Matthew 18:10.

Question: **Peter, what about the gospel? Are the angels interested in this too?**

Answer: "Unto whom it was revealed, that not unto themselves, but unto us they did minister the things, which are now reported unto you by them that have preached the gospel unto you with the Holy Ghost sent down from heaven; which things the angels desire to look into." 1 Peter 1:12.

Question: **Daniel, do angels assist man in understanding the Word of God?**

Answer: "Yea, whiles I was speaking in prayer, even the man Gabriel, whom I had seen in the vision at the beginning, being caused to fly swiftly, touched me about the time of the evening oblation. And he informed me, and talked with me, and said, O Daniel, I am now come forth to give thee skill and understanding." Daniel 9:21, 22.

Question: **David, do Christians enjoy the constant companionship of angels?**

Answer: "The angel of the Lord encampeth round about them that fear him, and delivereth them." Psalm 34:7.

Question: **Moses, what promise did the Lord make to the children of Israel?**

Answer: "Behold, I send an Angel before thee, to keep thee in the way, and to bring thee into the place which I have prepared." Exodus 23:20.

Question: **Luke, when Paul was in utmost danger, what happened?**

Answer: "There stood by me this night the angel of God, whose I am, and whom I serve, saying, Fear not, Paul; thou must be brought before Caesar: and, lo, God hath given thee all them that sail with thee." Acts 27:23, 24.

Question: **The angel did his job well. Not a soul was lost. Daniel, what happened when your jealous colleagues had you thrown into the lions' den?**

Answer: "My God hath sent his angel, and hath shut the

lions' mouths, that they have not hurt me: forasmuch as before him innocency was found in me; and also before thee, O king, have I done no hurt." Daniel 6:22.

Question: **In another study we mentioned evil angels. It is they who invaded and conquered mankind at the tree in Eden. Their sway would be planet-wide but for a counter-invasion. Please tell us about that.**

Answer: "Forasmuch then as the children are partakers of flesh and blood, he also himself likewise took part of the same; that through death he might destroy him that had the power of death, that is, the devil." Hebrews 2:14.

Question: **John, who will accomplish the binding of Satan?**

Answer: "I saw an angel come down from heaven, having the key of the bottomless pit and a great chain in his hand. And he laid hold on the dragon, that old serpent, which is the Devil, and Satan, and bound him a thousand years." Revelation 20:1, 2.

Question: **Daniel, as you look ahead what do you see for the sons of men?**

Answer: "At that time shall Michael stand up, the great prince which standeth for the children of thy people: and there shall be a time of trouble, such as never was since there was a nation even to that same time: and at that time thy people shall be delivered, every one that shall be found written in the book." Daniel 12:1.

Question: **Daniel tells of the deliverance of God's people. David, how will this be accomplished?**

Answer: "He shall give his angels charge over thee, to keep thee in all thy ways. They shall bear thee up in their hands, lest thou dash thy foot against a stone." Psalm 91:11, 12.

Question: **John, is it true that angels supervise the preaching of the gospel?**

Answer: "I saw another angel fly in the midst of heaven, having the everlasting gospel to preach unto them that dwell on the earth, and to every nation, and kindred, and tongue, and people." Revelation 14:6.

Question: **Two other heavenly messengers followed him. John, describe the climax of the gospel.**

Answer: "After these things I saw another angel come down from heaven, having great power; and the earth was lightened with his glory." Revelation 18:1.

Question: **By what means did the Lord send a message to the earth about the end of the longest time prophecy in the Bible?**

Answer: "The angel which I saw stand upon the sea and upon the earth lifted up his hand to heaven, and sware by him that liveth for ever and ever . . . that there should be time no longer." Revelation 10:5, 6.

Question: **In what was perhaps his most sacred mission, who announced to Mary that Christ would be born, Luke?**

Answer: "The angel came in unto her, and said, Hail, thou that art highly favoured, the Lord is with thee: blessed art thou among women." Luke 1:28.

Question: **Who made the announcement to the shepherds of the birth of their King?**

Answer: "There were in the same country shepherds abiding in the field, keeping watch over their flock by night. And, lo, the angel of the Lord came upon them, and the glory of the Lord shone round about them: and they were sore afraid. And the angel said unto them, Fear not: for, behold, I bring you good tidings of great joy, which shall be to all people." Luke 2:8-10.

Question: **When Herod sought to kill Jesus, who warned Joseph to flee into Egypt with the Child?**

Answer: "The angel of the Lord appeareth to Joseph in a dream, saying, Arise, and take the young child and his mother, and flee into Egypt, and be thou there until I bring thee word: for Herod will seek the young child to destroy him." Matthew 2:13.

Question: **After His terrible ordeal in the wilderness, Christ was exhausted. Matthew, what tender scene is opened to our view?**

Answer: "Then the devil leaveth him, and, behold, angels came and ministered unto him." Matthew 4:11.

Question: **In the agony of Gethsemane, when the bitter cup of man's second death trembled in the Saviour's hand, who was there to strengthen Him?**

Answer: "There appeared an angel unto him from heaven,

strengthening him." Luke 22:43.

Question: **In the moment of supreme crisis, how did Jesus express confidence in the angels?**

Answer: "Thinkest thou that I cannot now pray to my Father, and he shall presently give me more than twelve legions of angels?" Matthew 26:53.

Question: **Who appeared at His resurrection?**

Answer: "Behold, there was a great earthquake: for the angel of the Lord descended from heaven, and came and rolled back the stone from the door, and sat upon it." Matthew 28:2.

Question: **When Christ ascended to heaven, what chant did the angels raise inside and outside the New Jerusalem?**

Answer: "Lift up your heads, O ye gates; and be ye lift up, ye everlasting doors; and the King of glory shall come in. Who is this King of glory? The Lord strong and mighty, the Lord mighty in battle. . . . Who is this King of glory? The Lord of hosts, he is the King of glory." Psalm 24:7-10.

Question: **John, what majestic sight was yours in vision?**

Answer: "I saw heaven opened, and behold a white horse; and he that sat upon him was called Faithful and True, and in righteousness he doth judge and make war. . . . And he was clothed with a vesture dipped in blood: and his name is called The Word of God. And the armies which were in heaven followed him upon white horses, clothed in fine linen, white and clean." Revelation 19:11-14.

Question: **This is a description of the second coming of Christ. Matthew, can you add to this?**

Answer: "When the Son of man shall come in his glory, and all the holy angels with him, then shall he sit upon the throne of his glory: and before him shall be gathered all nations: and he shall separate them one from another, as a shepherd divideth his sheep from the goats." Matthew 25:31, 32.

Question: **What final glimpse do we get of the work of angels in the salvation of man, Matthew?**

Answer: "He shall send his angels with a great sound of a trumpet, and they shall gather together his elect from the four winds, from one end of heaven to the other." Matthew 24:31.

Thank you, gentlemen. This lesson leaves the Christian little to fear. In this we see the strong arm of the Lord laid bare. We can now testify with Job, "I know that thou canst do every thing, and that no thought can be withholden from thee." Job 42:2. And with King Darius we may exult, "In every dominion of my kingdom men tremble and fear before the God of Daniel: for he is the living God, and stedfast for ever, and his kingdom that which shall not be destroyed, and his dominion shall be even unto the end. He delivereth and rescueth, and he worketh signs and wonders in heaven and in earth, who hath delivered Daniel from the power of the lions." Daniel 6:26, 27.

> "Praise God, from whom all blessings flow;
> Praise Him, all creatures here below;
> Praise Him above, ye heavenly host;
> Praise Father, Son, and Holy Ghost."

The Return of Jesus

PAINTING BY CLYDE PROVONSHA   © BY REVIEW AND HERALD

One day man's wickedness will cause the destruction of this old world.
When that day comes, Christ will return to earth in power and glory to
make all things new.

10

The Return of Jesus

Jesus Christ, while on earth, made a clear promise to return to the earth. Where it is known, this promise brings joy to believers and dismay to the enemies of Jehovah. Both know what it will mean. For the righteous it is the fulfillment of a dream. For the wicked it is the end of a nightmare. The coming of the Lord is the new focal point in history. For the wicked, it is the chasm toward which the rapids flow. For the righteous, it is the golden gate to an eternity of joy. But how will He come? How will His coming affect the earth, the nations, and all nature? We turn to the prophets for the answers, for that event must not come upon us unawares.

Question: **John, did Jesus make a definite promise to return to this earth?**

Answer: "If I go and prepare a place for you, I will come again, and receive you unto myself; that where I am, there ye may be also." John 14:3.

Question: **Luke, did He go away? What did the angels say?**

Answer: "Ye men of Galilee, why stand ye gazing up into heaven? this same Jesus, which is taken up from you into heaven, shall so come in like manner as ye have seen him go into heaven." Acts 1:11.

Question: **Why did He go away?**

Answer: "Christ is not entered into the holy places made with hands, which are the figures of the true; but into heaven itself, now to appear in the presence of God for us." Hebrews 9:24.

Question: **Interesting. We will come back to this in a later dis-**

cussion. But Christ is still working for our salvation, though now in heaven. What matchless love! Why will Jesus come again? What reason did He give, John?

Answer: "Behold, I come quickly; and my reward is with me, to give every man according as his work shall be." Revelation 22:12.

Question: **Many good people who served the Lord will have died before His second coming. Will they sleep through this blessed event? This question is for you, Paul.**

Answer: "The Lord himself shall descend from heaven with a shout, with the voice of the archangel, and with the trump of God: and the dead in Christ shall rise first." 1 Thessalonians 4:16.

Question: **Also, many wicked people will have died before the coming of Christ. John, will they too awaken?**

Answer: "The rest of the dead lived not again until the thousand years were finished." Revelation 20:5.

Question: **Are you saying that only the righteous dead will be raised at the second coming of Christ?**

Answer: "Blessed and holy is he that hath part in the first resurrection: on such the second death hath no power, but they shall be priests of God and of Christ, and shall reign with him a thousand years." Revelation 20:6.

Question: **Will some of the wicked be raised at this time to see our Lord return in glory? John, you wrote concerning this.**

Answer: "Behold, he cometh with clouds; and every eye shall see him, and they also which pierced him: and all kindreds of the earth shall wail because of him." Revelation 1:7.

Question: **Daniel, did you foresee the resurrection of a special group of the wicked at the second coming of the Lord?**

Answer: "And many of them that sleep in the dust of the earth shall awake, some to everlasting life, and some to shame and everlasting contempt." Daniel 12:2.

Question: **Good, Daniel and John! You agree that not all the dead will be raised at the second coming of Christ, but that all the righteous and some of the wicked will come forth. Matthew, how will the righteous be gathered in that day?**

Answer: "He shall send his angels with a great sound of a

trumpet, and they shall gather together his elect from the four winds, from one end of heaven to the other." Matthew 24:31.

Question: **Matthew, what did Jesus say of the secret rapture theory of His coming? Did He teach this?**

Answer: "Then if any man shall say unto you, Lo, here is Christ, or there; believe it not. Wherefore if they shall say unto you, Behold, he is in the desert; go not forth: behold, he is in the secret chambers; believe it not." Matthew 24:23, 26.

Question: **That disposes of both Spiritualism and the theory of a secret return of our Lord to the earth. Matthew, did Jesus ever plainly say that His return would be a literal, visible event?**

Answer: "As the lightning cometh out of the east, and shineth even unto the west; so shall also the coming of the Son of man be." Matthew 24:27.

Question: **That is plain enough. But, Paul, you describe the coming of Christ as a thief, don't you?**

Answer: "Yourselves know perfectly that the day of the Lord so cometh as a thief in the night." 1 Thessalonians 5:2.

Question: **Paul, are you contradicting Jesus? Are you saying that Christ will come secretly?**

Answer: "The Lord himself shall descend from heaven with a shout, with the voice of the archangel, and with the trump of God: and the dead in Christ shall rise first." 1 Thessalonians 4:16.

Question: **So you agree with Christ and the prophets that His return will be a public, earth-shaking event. In what sense, then, will it be like a thief in the night?**

Answer: "When they shall say, Peace and safety; then sudden destruction cometh upon them, as travail upon a woman with child; and they shall not escape." 1 Thessalonians 5:3.

Question: **That is clear. It will be *public,* but like a thief it will be *unexpected.* Matthew, does Jesus support Paul in this?**

Answer: "Watch therefore: for ye know not what hour your Lord doth come. But know this, that if the goodman of the house had known in what watch the thief would come, he would have watched, and would not have suffered his house to be broken up. Therefore be ye also ready: for in such an hour as ye think not the Son of man cometh." Matthew 24:42-44.

Question: **How will men in general greet the coming of Christ? Matthew, give us the words of Jesus.**

Answer: "Then shall appear the sign of the Son of man in heaven: and then shall all the tribes of the earth mourn, and they shall see the Son of man coming in the clouds of heaven with power and great glory." Matthew 24:30.

Question: **John, you have also described many running from the presence of the Lord, have you not?**

Answer: "The kings of the earth, and the great men, and the rich men, and the chief captains, and the mighty men, and every bondman, and every free man, hid themselves in the dens and in the rocks of the mountains; and said to the mountains and rocks, Fall on us, and hide us from the face of him that sitteth on the throne, and from the wrath of the Lamb." Revelation 6:15, 16.

Question: **Quite a distinguished class of people running from the Lord. How sad! What will the righteous say, Isaiah?**

Answer: "He will swallow up death in victory; and the Lord God will wipe away tears from off all faces; and the rebuke of his people shall he take away from off all the earth: for the Lord hath spoken it. And it shall be said in that day, Lo, this is our God; we have waited for him, and he will save us: this is the Lord; we have waited for him, we will be glad and rejoice in his salvation." Isaiah 25:8, 9.

Question: **John, what will happen when Jesus comes?**

Answer: "And the heaven departed as a scroll when it is rolled together; and every mountain and island were moved out of their places." Revelation 6:14.

Question: **Isaiah, have you anything to add to this?**

Answer: "Behold, the Lord maketh the earth empty, and maketh it waste, and turneth it upside down, and scattereth abroad the inhabitants thereof." Isaiah 24:1.

Question: **Jeremiah, how horrible will be the end of the living wicked at the coming of Christ?**

Answer: "Thus saith the Lord of hosts, Behold, evil shall go forth from nation to nation, and a great whirlwind shall be raised up from the coasts of the earth. And the slain of the Lord shall be at that day from one end of the earth even unto the other end of the earth: they shall not be lamented, neither gathered, nor buried; they shall be dung upon the ground.'' Jeremiah 25:32, 33.

Question: **Matthew, did Jesus provide any clue by which we might determine the day and hour of His coming?**

Answer: ''Of that day and hour knoweth no man, no, not the angels of heaven, but my Father only.'' Matthew 24:36.

Question: **That settles it. But may we not at least know when His coming is near? Did Christ give some clue?**

Answer: ''Immediately after the tribulation of those days shall the sun be darkened, and the moon shall not give her light, and the stars shall fall from heaven, and the powers of the heavens shall be shaken.'' Matthew 24:29.

Question: **History says that most of these prophecies have already been fulfilled. The stars fell November 13, 1833, and the sun grew mysteriously dark on May 19, 1780, and the next night the moon appeared as blood. The Lord's coming must be near. Matthew, did our Lord give any other signs?**

Answer: ''As in the days that were before the flood they were eating and drinking, marrying and giving in marriage, until the day that Noe entered into the ark, and knew not until the flood came, and took them all away; so shall also the coming of the Son of man be.'' Matthew 24:38, 39.

Question: **Immorality, gluttony, and drunkenness have all reached alarming proportions. Things cannot continue much longer. Christ's coming is near. Luke, did Jesus speak of agitation among nations?**

Answer: ''Take heed to yourselves, lest at any time your hearts be overcharged with surfeiting, and drunkenness, and cares of this life, and so that day come upon you unawares. For as a snare shall it come on all them that dwell on the face of the whole earth. Watch ye therefore, and pray always, that ye may be accounted worthy to escape all these things that shall come to pass, and to stand before the Son of man.'' Luke 21:34-36.

Thank you, gentlemen, for this enlightening interview. The tempo of the times increases as our mad world rushes toward its date with destiny—a face-to-face confrontation between man and his Maker. Precious hours of probation are ticking away. The slowly falling grains of sand in the hourglass of time are well-nigh spent. But the voice of God is still heard in the earth; His hand of mercy beckons. Won't you, dear reader, heed His voice and grasp His hand *right now?*

Christ's death on the cross speaks to us of the infinite love of God, and of His concern for us in our lost condition. His death made eternal life possible for us, by faith in His atoning sacrifice.

The Cross

II

The Cross

On lonely Golgotha three men died, two of them thieves. One died *in* his sins; the other died *to* his sins. On the middle cross was Christ. He died *for* sin—our sins and those of the whole world. His cross stands astride human history as man's supreme crisis. The destiny of all mankind was decided there. To live or die, survive or perish, are the issues the cross of Christ poses for every man.

But even more was settled here. Lucifer, the archfiend, was on that hill. This was his last chance to wring from the lips of the Son of God one curse, one complaint, one minor concession. What demons had failed to do in thirty-three years they must now do in a few minutes. In reckless desperation they went about their task that day. Success or failure was a matter of hours.

The cross settled forever the unanswered questions of their minds. It could therefore be said of Calvary as of Bethlehem, "The hopes and fears of all the years/Are met in thee tonight." Here justice and mercy kissed each other. Here apparent defeat was ultimate victory. Here the shedding of blood was remission of sins. The disappointed disciples, cowering in the grim grip of doubt, might even then have, like the "morning stars," sung together, and like "all the sons of God," shouted for joy.

Let us focus the wisdom of the prophets on the cross for the conversion of sinners and the confirming of saints.

Question: **At what point in history was man first promised a Saviour from sin?**

Answer: "I will put enmity between thee and the woman, and between thy seed and her seed; it shall bruise thy head, and thou shalt bruise his heel." Genesis 3:15.

90

Question: **That Lucifer, the serpent, would bruise the Saviour's heel is the first promise to man of the crisis of the cross. Tell us, Moses, what precious promise did Jacob utter concerning the coming Messiah?**

Answer: "The sceptre shall not depart from Judah, nor a lawgiver from between his feet, until Shiloh come; and unto him shall the gathering of the people be." Genesis 49:10.

Question: **Tell us, John, what alone could be the reason for the sacrifice of Christ?**

Answer: "God so loved the world, that he gave his only begotten Son, that whosoever believeth in him should not perish, but have everlasting life." John 3:16.

Question: **Paul, do you agree?**

Answer: "God commendeth his love toward us, in that, while we were yet sinners, Christ died for us." Romans 5:8.

Question: **What, in reality, did the death of Christ accomplish for man?**

Answer: "God was in Christ, reconciling the world unto himself, not imputing their trespasses unto them; and hath committed unto us the word of reconciliation." 2 Corinthians 5:19.

Question: **So, then, it was all for us, Paul?**

Answer: "Ye know the grace of our Lord Jesus Christ, that, though he was rich, yet for your sakes he became poor, that ye through his poverty might be rich." 2 Corinthians 8:9.

Question: **Could the human family be redeemed by any other means?**

Answer: "Neither is there salvation in any other: for there is none other name under heaven given among men, whereby we must be saved." Acts 4:12.

Question: **Why is this so, Paul?**

Answer: "For by him were all things created, that are in heaven, and that are in earth, visible and invisible, whether they be thrones, or dominions, or principalities, or powers: all things were created by him, and for him." Colossians 1:16.

Question: **That is clear. Only the Creator could redeem His creation. Luke, how was it possible for the Creator to give His life as a sacrifice?**

Answer: "The angel answered and said unto her [Mary], The

Holy Ghost shall come upon thee, and the power of the Highest shall overshadow thee: therefore also that holy thing which shall be born of thee shall be called the Son of God.'' Luke 1:35.

Question: **Do we presume then that Christ became physically akin to the human family?**
Answer: "In all things it behoved him to be made like unto his brethren, that he might be a merciful and faithful high priest in things pertaining to God, to make reconciliation for the sins of the people." Hebrews 2:17.

Question: **Being made like unto us, He could relate to us. Good. What is said of the time of His incarnation?**
Answer: "When the fulness of the time was come, God sent forth his Son, made of a woman, made under the law." Galatians 4:4.

Question: **The time was ripe, for man was culturally corrupt, politically sterile, and spiritually dead. For what did Christ say He had come?**
Answer: "The thief cometh not, but for to steal, and to kill, and to destroy: I am come that they might have life, and that they might have it more abundantly." John 10:10.

Question: **Good, John, but does this refer to the present world or the one to come?**
Answer: "There is no man that hath left house, or parents, or brethren, or wife, or children, for the kingdom of God's sake, who shall not receive manifold more in this present time, and in the world to come life everlasting." Luke 18:29, 30.

Question: **What was Christ's own announced purpose in coming here?**
Answer: "The Son of man is come to seek and to save that which was lost." Luke 19:10.

Question: **John, does God the Father agree with this?**
Answer: "For God sent not his Son into the world to condemn the world; but that the world through him might be saved." John 3:17.

Question: **How crucial a matter is it to have faith in Him?**
Answer: "He that believeth on the Son hath everlasting life: and he that believeth not the Son shall not see life; but the wrath of God abideth on him." John 3:36.

Question: **Mark, where did they crucify Jesus?**

Answer: "They bring him unto the place Golgotha, which is, being interpreted, The place of a skull." Mark 15:22.

Question: **Mark, please continue. Tell us what happened there.**

Answer: "And they gave him to drink wine mingled with myrrh: but he received it not. And when they had crucified him, they parted his garments, casting lots upon them, what every man should take. And it was the third hour, and they crucified him." Mark 15:23-25.

Question: **Isaiah, can you add to this?**

Answer: "He was oppressed, and he was afflicted, yet he opened not his mouth: he is brought as a lamb to the slaughter, and as a sheep before her shearers is dumb, so he openeth not his mouth. . . . And he made his grave with the wicked, and with the rich in his death; because he had done no violence, neither was any deceit in his mouth." Isaiah 53:7-9.

Question: **Isaiah, why did He die?**

Answer: "For the transgression of my people was he stricken." Isaiah 53:8.

Question: **Peter, do you agree with Isaiah?**

Answer: "Who his own self bare our sins in his own body on the tree, that we, being dead to sins, should live unto righteousness: by whose stripes ye were healed." 1 Peter 2:24.

Question: **Wonderful Jesus! He paid the price for our sins on the cross. Tell us, Peter, may we now escape the penalty of transgression?**

Answer: "Christ also hath once suffered for sins, the just for the unjust, that he might bring us to God, being put to death in the flesh, but quickened by the Spirit." 1 Peter 3:18.

Question: **Matthew, what should our response be to such matchless love?**

Answer: "Jesus said unto him, Thou shalt love the Lord thy God with all thy heart, and with all thy soul, and with all thy mind." Matthew 22:37.

Question: **Paul, how hopeless was our condition, and by contrast, how has Christ changed this?**

Answer: "Ye were without Christ, being aliens from the commonwealth of Israel, and strangers from the covenants of promise, having no hope, and without God in the world: but now in Christ Jesus ye who sometimes were far off are made nigh by the blood of Christ." Ephesians 2:12, 13.

Question: **Now, gentlemen, let us consider the specific accomplishments of the cross of Christ. John, what did Jesus say?**

Answer: "Whosoever believeth in him should not perish, but have everlasting life." John 3:16.

Question: **Christ's death at Calvary was my "second death." None of us need to burn in hell. Christ suffered hell at the hands of men and demons in our stead. John, give us another accomplishment of the cross.**

Answer: "If we confess our sins, he is faithful and just to forgive us our sins, and to cleanse us from all unrighteousness." 1 John 1:9.

Question: **We may actually master our weaknesses by the cleansing of the blood. Good. Isaiah, can you add to this?**

Answer: "Seek ye the Lord while he may be found, call ye upon him while he is near: let the wicked forsake his way, and the unrighteous man his thoughts: and let him return unto the Lord, and he will have mercy upon him; and to our God, for he will abundantly pardon." Isaiah 55:6, 7.

Question: **We are not only cleansed but pardoned. Thank God! Paul, you have another thought.**

Answer: "The grace of God that bringeth salvation hath appeared to all men, teaching us that, denying ungodliness and worldly lusts, we should live soberly, righteously, and godly, in this present world." Titus 2:11, 12.

Question: **So, Paul, you add *strength* to pardon and cleansing. Luke, what have you to say?**

Answer: "Take heed therefore unto yourselves, and to all the flock, over the which the Holy Ghost hath made you overseers, to feed the church of God, which he hath purchased with his own blood." Acts 20:28.

Question: **We are bought back from the enemy by the blood of Christ; ransomed from the hand of the kidnaper. Paul, you have an important observation.**

Answer: "Whom God hath set forth to be a propitiation through faith in his blood, to declare his righteousness for the remission of sins that are past, through the forbearance of God.'' Romans 3:25.

Question: **So His blood fully satisfied the penalty for sin. The death of Christ also declares that the law must be obeyed. For it was the broken law that required a sacrifice. Rather than change His law, Christ took man's place and bowed to its *claims*, which were in fact His own. So we may agree with Paul's important conclusion, may we not?**

Answer: "Having made peace through the blood of his cross, by him to reconcile all things unto himself; by him, I say, whether they be things in earth, or things in heaven.'' Colossians 1:20.

Question: **Moses, when the plagues smote Egypt, how was the death of the Israelite firstborn avoided?**

Answer: "The blood shall be to you for a token upon the houses where ye are: and when I see the blood, I will pass over you, and the plague shall not be upon you to destroy you, when I smite the land of Egypt.'' Exodus 12:13.

Question: **Moses, what animal was used for the blood of deliverance?**

Answer: "Then Moses called for all the elders of Israel, and said unto them, Draw out and take you a lamb according to your families, and kill the passover.'' Exodus 12:21.

Question: **Of whom was this lamb a symbol?**

Answer: "The next day John seeth Jesus coming unto him, and saith, Behold the Lamb of God, which taketh away the sin of the world.'' John 1:29.

Question: **On Golgotha that day, most of His disciples had fled, but John remained. How did Jesus show His solicitude for His mother and appreciation for, and to, John?**

Answer: "When Jesus therefore saw his mother, and the disciple standing by, whom he loved, he saith unto his mother, Woman, behold thy son! Then saith he to the disciple, Behold thy mother! And from that hour that disciple took her unto his own home.'' John 19:26, 27.

Question: **Though dying Himself, how did Jesus show His sensitivity to the repentant thief?**

Answer: "He said unto Jesus, Lord, remember me when

thou comest into thy kingdom. And Jesus said unto him, Verily I say unto thee, To day shalt thou be with me in paradise.'' Luke 23:42, 43.

Question: **What was Jesus' dying attitude toward His enemies?**
Answer: "Then said Jesus, Father, forgive them; for they know not what they do." Luke 23:34.

Question: **At about the ninth hour—three o'clock in the afternoon—what happened?**
Answer: "When Jesus had cried with a loud voice, he said, Father, into thy hands I commend my spirit: and having said thus, he gave up the ghost." Luke 23:46.

Question: **How did nature itself respond at this dramatic moment?**
Answer: "From the sixth hour there was darkness over all the land unto the ninth hour. . . . And the earth did quake, and the rocks rent." Matthew 27:45-51.

Question: **They buried our Lord in a newly hewn tomb, and there He lay in sweet repose until the morning of the first day of the week. Tell us, Matthew, what happened then?**
Answer: "Behold, there was a great earthquake: for the angel of the Lord descended from heaven, and came and rolled back the stone from the door, and sat upon it. His countenance was like lightning, and his raiment white as snow: and for fear of him the keepers did shake, and became as dead men. And the angel answered and said unto the women, Fear not ye: for I know that ye seek Jesus, which was crucified. He is not here: for he is risen, as he said. Come, see the place where the Lord lay." Matthew 28:2-6.

I sit in wonderment at the events traced in this vital chapter. Mingled emotions grip me as I pen this conclusion. Is it possible that joy and sorrow, pleasure and pain, hope and fear, and a smile be mingled with a tear in a single heart at the same moment? How else can one describe repentant joy?

Golgotha, hill of a thousand tears, birthplace of a million anthems. The cross, symbol of our shame and cradle of our hope, the end. But not the end; the beginning. Yes, the beginning of a new life in Christ for you today.

The Law That
Foretold the Future

12

The Law That
Foretold the Future

The ceremonial law has been little studied and seldom understood. And yet its significance to the plan of salvation cannot be denied. The sacrificial system pointed forward to Christ. It was the gospel in the Old Testament. It described the mission of Christ in the world and prefigured His passion and priestly ministry. From the animal offerings of Abel's day to the sophisticated services of Solomon's Temple, the ceremonial law had as its chief function to supply what the violated Decalogue demanded—the death of the sinner or his substitute, and the administration of the benefits of that sacrifice. The ceremonial law promised a Saviour and fed the hope of God's people during their long journey through history toward Bethlehem and the Incarnation.

We turn to the prophets for this revelation of grace in the Old Testament. To familiarize oneself with the ceremonial law is to study the doctrine of salvation by grace through faith in the Lord Jesus.

Question: **Moses, in the book of the law, which you wrote, I understand that there is a law separate from the Ten Commandments which we call ceremonial. How did you dramatize this difference?**

Answer: "And it came to pass, when Moses had made an end of writing the words of this law in a book, until they were finished, that Moses commanded the Levites, which bare the ark of the covenant of the Lord, saying, Take this book of the law, and put it in the side of the ark of the covenant of the Lord your God, that it may be there for a witness against thee." Deuteronomy 31:24-26.

Question: **Where did you put the Ten Commandments?**

Answer: "I turned myself and came down from the mount, and put the tables in the ark which I had made." Deuteronomy 10:5.

Question: **Moses, God told you to write the ceremonial law, but what of the Ten Commandments?**

Answer: "He [God] gave unto Moses, when he had made an end of communing with him upon mount Sinai, two tables of testimony, tables of stone, written with the finger of God." Exodus 31:18.

Question: **Why was the ceremonial law added? Paul, have you the answer?**

Answer: "Wherefore then serveth the law? It was added because of transgressions, till the seed should come to whom the promise was made; and it was ordained by angels in the hand of a mediator." Galatians 3:19.

Question: **So the ceremonial law was added because of the transgression of the ten-commandment law. Interesting. But tell me, what were the ceremonial laws designed to do?**

Answer: "Wherefore the law was our schoolmaster to bring us unto Christ, that we might be justified by faith." Galatians 3:24.

Question: **In what sense did the ceremonial laws "bring" people to Christ?**

Answer: "Let no man therefore judge you in meat, or in drink, or in respect of an holyday, or of the new moon, or of the sabbath days: which are a shadow of things to come; but the body is of Christ." Colossians 2:16, 17.

Question: **So the ceremonial laws pointed forward to Christ. They prefigured Him. Is this why they were blotted out when Christ died on the cross, Paul?**

Answer: "Blotting out the handwriting of ordinances that was against us, which was contrary to us, and took it out of the way, nailing it to his cross." Colossians 2:14.

Question: **Since the ceremonial law represents Christ, I can understand why it ceased at the cross. Shadow must ever yield to substance. But tell me, Paul, what do you mean when you say, "Let no man therefore judge you in meat, or in drink"? Are you here discussing diet?**

Answer: "Wherefore come out from among them, and be ye separate, saith the Lord, and touch not the unclean thing; and I will receive you." 2 Corinthians 6:17.

Question: **So, Paul, you hold that Biblical restrictions on diet are still binding—"touch not the unclean thing"? But, Luke, tell us, was it the New Testament custom to abstain from unclean foods? What significant admission did Peter make?**

Answer: "Peter said, Not so, Lord; for I have never eaten any thing that is common or unclean." Acts 10:14.

Question: **We know, of course, that the animals in Peter's vision represented people, and that God was trying to break down prejudice in Peter, but at this point in the vision Peter didn't understand this. At first he thought the message had to do with eating habits. But why were the sacrificial offerings made?**

Answer: "The law having a shadow of good things to come, and not the very image of the things, can never with those sacrifices which they offered year by year continually make the comers thereunto perfect." Hebrews 10:1.

Question: **You say these offerings had a "shadow of good things to come." That is familiar language. These offerings for sin did not secure *actual remission* of sin, but pointed to Christ, whose death indeed would do so. Thus the ceremonial law led the precrucifixion sinner to Christ. Do you agree?**

Answer: "And every priest standeth daily ministering and offering oftentimes the same sacrifices, which can never take away sins: but this man, after he had offered one sacrifice for sins for ever, sat down on the right hand of God." Hebrews 10:11, 12.

Question: **Then the earthly offering tutored the sinner concerning the one great offering at Calvary—that of Christ Himself. Will the blood of Christ cleanse from sin, thus fulfilling the promise of the ceremonial sacrifices? John, will you answer?**

Answer: "But if we walk in the light, as he is in the light, we have fellowship one with another, and the blood of Jesus Christ his Son cleanseth us from all sin." 1 John 1:7.

Question: **Why was the blood of goats and calves used in the service of the earthly tabernacle, Paul?**

Answer: "It was therefore necessary that the patterns of

things in the heavens should be purified with these." Hebrews 9:23.

Question: **But of what was this symbolic cleansing a figure?**

Answer: "Christ is not entered into the holy places made with hands, which are the figures of the true; but into heaven itself, now to appear in the presence of God for us." Hebrews 9:24.

Question: **Please give us a direct comparison of what the ceremonial offerings accomplished, and what Christ accomplishes. Make it plain!**

Answer: "If the blood of bulls and of goats, and the ashes of an heifer sprinkling the unclean, sanctifieth to the purifying of the flesh: how much more shall the blood of Christ, who through the eternal Spirit offered himself without spot to God, purge your conscience from dead works to serve the living God?" Hebrews 9:13, 14.

Question: **Since these ceremonial requirements served only one purpose—to point to Christ's atoning sacrifice and priestly ministry—what happened to them when Jesus died?**

Answer: "Then said he, Lo, I come to do thy will, O God. He taketh away the first, that he may establish the second." Hebrews 10:9.

Question: **That is understandable. The "second" is the fulfillment of the "first." The shadow is no longer important when we have the real thing. We deprive ourselves of the benefits of living reality by clinging to less meaningful ritual. The ritual thus becomes "against us." Would you agree, Paul?**

Answer: "Blotting out the handwriting of ordinances that was against us, which was contrary to us, and took it out of the way, nailing it to his cross." Colossians 2:14.

Question: **When people allow "the shadow of things to come" to cause them to reject Him to whom the shadow points, the shadow or ceremony becomes "contrary to us." Paul, to the people before the cross the ceremonial services of the Temple pointed forward to the cross and priestly ministry of Christ. We live this side of the crucifixion. What service was instituted by our Lord to remind us that Christ died for our sins?**

Answer: "The Lord Jesus the same night in which he was betrayed took bread: and when he had given thanks, he brake it, and said, Take, eat: this is my body, which is broken for you: this do in remembrance of me." 1 Corinthians 11:23, 24.

Question: **The meat offering pointed forward to the piercing of the body of Christ, while the broken bread of the communion table points back to the fact of the crucifixion. Both symbols were designed to strengthen man's faith—one in an *event* that was to come; the other in the *same event* now past as it relates to the priestly ministry of Christ. Paul, I believe you have more to say.**

Answer: "After the same manner also he took the cup, when he had supped, saying, This cup is the new testament in my blood: this do ye, as oft as ye drink it, in remembrance of me." 1 Corinthians 11:25.

Question: **Then would you agree that the drink offering of the ceremonial ritual, which pointed forward to the shedding of blood at Calvary, is similar to the communion wine that points back to the fact of Christ's sacrifice? This is clear. It seems, therefore, that as with the people before the crucifixion, those since that event also have a problem of faith. The God of heaven knew that without a schoolmaster man would forget, so He gave the ceremonial law to keep alive the faith of His people in an event to come. But what of the Ten Commandments, James? Is it a serious matter to disregard them?**

Answer: "Whosoever shall keep the whole law, and yet offend in one point, he is guilty of all." James 2:10.

Question: **But some consider the restrictions of the law a burden. James, are they correct in this?**

Answer: "Whoso looketh into the perfect law of liberty, and continueth therein, he being not a forgetful hearer, but a doer of the work, this man shall be blessed in his deed." James 1:25.

Question: **So it is a law of liberty, just the opposite of what some think. Matthew, did Jesus comment on this?**

Answer: "Come unto me, all ye that labour and are heavy laden, and I will give you rest. Take my yoke upon you, and learn of me; for I am meek and lowly in heart: and ye shall find rest unto your souls." Matthew 11:28, 29.

Christ is the answer to the problem of obedience. Give Him first place in your heart, and He will bring all the richness and joy imaginable into the obedience experience. When we come to Him daily in childlike faith, He will fill our hearts with His love, and His law becomes to us a way of life.

The Law of God

13

The Law of God

There are five great divisions of law in the Bible—the Ten Commandments, the ceremonial law, civil law, laws of health, and the laws of nature. In addition, the word *law* as used in the Bible often means either the first books of the Bible (the Pentateuch) or God's will as revealed in the Old Testament.

There is little doubt that the civil laws of the Scriptures ceased their function when the nation of Israel came to an end. We know that natural law is still operative in the universe and on this planet. In another discussion we will deal with the health laws of the Bible and our relationship to them. In this and following chapters we shall talk about the moral and ceremonial laws. These two great laws are related, yet separate. Is the law of God still binding upon Christians? Or, as some teach, has all law lost its force? Again we turn to the prophets for answers. Thus far we have not been disappointed.

Question: **Moses, were men saved in Old Testament times by keeping the law?**

Answer: No, for "Noah found grace in the eyes of the Lord." Genesis 6:8.

Question: **Paul, Moses answered with an example. Could you give us a broader statement?**

Answer: "The grace of God that bringeth salvation hath appeared to all men, teaching us that, denying ungodliness and worldly lusts, we should live soberly, righteously, and godly, in this present world." Titus 2:11, 12.

Question: **So men in all ages have been saved by the unmerited favor of Christ? Good. Then what was the function of law in history, whether moral or ceremonial?**

Answer: "The law was our schoolmaster to bring us unto Christ, that we might be justified by faith. But after that faith is come, we are no longer under a schoolmaster." Galatians 3:24, 25.

Question: **God has been the teacher of His people, and through the ages the law and the prophets were His instruments of instruction. Can you confirm this, Luke?**
Answer: "The law and the prophets were until John: since that time the kingdom of God is preached, and every man presseth into it." Luke 16:16.

Question: **Matthew, does this mean that the Ten Commandments *ended* at the coming of John? What did Jesus say?**
Answer: "Think not that I am come to destroy the law [the writings of Moses], or the prophets: I am not come to destroy, but to fulfil. For verily I say unto you, Till heaven and earth pass, one jot or one tittle shall in no wise pass from the law, till all be fulfilled." Matthew 5:17, 18.

Question: **That is clear. But does this mean that we must observe all ten of the commandments while the heavens are above earth?**
Answer: "Whosoever therefore shall break one of these least commandments, and shall teach men so, he shall be called the least in the kingdom of heaven: but whosoever shall do and teach them, the same shall be called great in the kingdom of heaven." Matthew 5:19.

Question: **Then not even the coming of Christ abolished the Ten Commandments?**
Answer: "It is easier for heaven and earth to pass, than one tittle of the law to fail." Luke 16:17.

Question: **Now we know that before Adam sinned man had the privilege of face-to-face communication with God, but that thereafter He largely communicated His will through the law and the prophets. How long was this to last?**
Answer: "The law was our schoolmaster to bring us unto Christ that we might be justified by faith. But after that faith is come, we are no longer under a schoolmaster." Galatians 3:24, 25.

Question: **Then the law that God had given served as a school-**

master or tutor, spanning the time between Mount Sinai and the coming of Christ. But with the coming of Christ, face-to-face communication with Christ was briefly restored, and Christ *resumed in person this function of the law* as an "in person" expositor! Glorious thought! But is it correct, Matthew?

Answer: "While he yet spake, behold, a bright cloud overshadowed them: and behold a voice out of the cloud, which said, This is my beloved Son, in whom I am well pleased; hear ye him." Matthew 17:5.

Question: It is understandable that both the law (the writings of Moses) and prophets would yield to the greater Teacher the function of primary instruction, as indeed they did. But what statement by the Jews clearly indicates that they did not recognize this glorious fact of the divine living Teacher among them or its significance?

Answer: "Then they reviled him, and said, Thou art his disciple; but we are Moses' disciples. We know that God spake unto Moses: as for this fellow, we know not from whence he is." John 9:28, 29.

Question: "This fellow" indeed! There is every indication that the Jews in general chose to regard Christ as an ordinary man like other men. But in this way they were frustrated again and again. Tell us, Matthew, did the living Schoolmaster exempt man from obedience to the Ten Commandments?

Answer: "Ye have heard that it was said by them of old time, Thou shalt not kill; and whosoever shall kill shall be in danger of the judgment: but I say unto you, That whosoever is angry with his brother without a cause shall be in danger of the judgment." Matthew 5:21, 22.

Question: This strengthens the force of law, in that it reaches the heart, or attitude, of man. Did Jesus say more?

Answer: "Ye have heard that it was said by them of old time, Thou shalt not commit adultery: but I say unto you, That whosoever looketh on a woman to lust after her hath committed adultery with her already in his heart." Matthew 5:27, 28.

Question: This magnifies the law and opens up new depths of knowledge and concern. The new Schoolmaster was, in fact, man's Teacher in Eden. He was the giver of the law, and the inspiration of the prophets in all ages. He has greatly amplified His law by these two statements. Paul, aside from the tutor function which naturally Christ Himself assumed, what other function does the law perform now and ever?

Answer: "What shall we say then? Is the law sin? God forbid. Nay, I had not known sin, but by the law: for I had not known lust, except the law had said, Thou shalt not covet." Romans 7:7.

Question: **The law defines sin and thus shows us our need of Christ. Good answer. But how does this work?**

Answer: "But sin, that it might appear sin, working death in me by that which is good; that sin by the commandment might become exceeding sinful." Romans 7:13.

Question: **So the law becomes the God-given prosecutor to bring home to us the exceeding sinfulness of sin. This vital need the law supplies. But is there no deliverance from the guilt that sin, exposed by the law, produces in us?**

Answer: "I am crucified with Christ: nevertheless I live; yet not I, but Christ liveth in me: and the life which I now live in the flesh I live by the faith of the Son of God, who loved me, and gave himself for me." Galatians 2:20.

Question: **Thus the law no more condemns me, for I am converted to Christ, who forgives my sins and changes my heart and attitude, bringing my life into harmony with God's moral law. What else did Paul say on the subject?**

Answer: "Ye also are become dead to the law by the body of Christ; that ye should be married to another, even to him who is raised from the dead, that we should bring forth fruit unto God." Romans 7:4.

Question: **So, Paul, when you speak of being "free from the law," you mean free from its condemnation?**

Answer: "There is therefore now no condemnation to them which are in Christ Jesus, who walk not after the flesh, but after the Spirit." Romans 8:1.

Question: **So, under the new experience, it is not the law that changes, but man! The sin the law exposes must be *renounced.* The sinner must die with Christ. He must be *converted!* This lifts him out of the laws of condemnation into the sunlight of divine favor. But tell us, Paul, what should be the attitude of a new convert toward the law of God?**

Answer: "I delight in the law of God after the inward man." Romans 7:22.

Question: **Paul, how does the law of God become a part of day-to-day living?**

Answer: "What the law could not do in that it was weak through the flesh, God sending his own Son in the likeness of sinful flesh, and for sin, condemned sin in the flesh: that the righteousness of the law might be fulfilled in us, who walk not after the flesh, but after the Spirit." Romans 8:3, 4.

Question: **Then you would say, Paul, that a born-again Christian will obey the law of God?**

Answer: "Not the hearers of the law are just before God, but the doers of the law shall be justified." Romans 2:13.

Question: **But, Paul, some have felt that faith in Christ takes the place of obedience to His law. Is this true?**

Answer: "Do we then make void the law through faith? God forbid: yea, we establish the law." Romans 3:31.

Question: **But others think that grace exempts them from obedience to the Ten Commandments. Is this your teaching, Paul?**

Answer: "What shall we say then? Shall we continue in sin, that grace may abound? God forbid. How shall we, that are dead to sin, live any longer therein?" Romans 6:1, 2.

Question: **But the Bible says that love fulfills the law. What does this mean, John? What explanation does Jesus give?**

Answer: "If ye love me, keep my commandments." John 14:15.

Question: **That is clear. In the Christian, love for Christ produces obedience to God's law. Obedience is an act of love, not forced but natural. Those who love God obey Him. Wonderful. But is this also true of faith? James, help us.**

Answer: "Yea, a man may say, Thou hast faith, and I have works; shew me thy faith without thy works, and I will shew thee my faith by my works. Thou believest that there is one God; thou doest well: the devils also believe, and tremble. But wilt thou know, O vain man, that faith without works is dead?" James 2:18-20.

Question: **An important point! Obedience is a manifestation of faith. It is a natural outgrowth of trust. Obedience is an expres-**

sion of confidence in God performed in us by His sanctifying power. It is required not as a condition of salvation but as evidence that a person has been saved. The Christian obeys, not because he *must,* though indeed he must, but because he loves his Lord and his neighbor as himself. Thank God for the truth! But, Paul, some believe that obedience to the law puts a man against the promises of God. Is this true?

Answer: "Is the law then against the promises of God? God forbid." Galatians 3:21.

Question: Tell us, Moses, is this concept of obedience peculiar to the New Testament? I mean the love concept.

Answer: "Hear, O Israel: The Lord our God is one Lord: and thou shalt love the Lord thy God with all thine heart, and with all thy soul, and with all thy might." Deuteronomy 6:4, 5.

Question: So obedience, even in Old Testament times, sprang from love to God. But what about one's fellow man, Moses? Surely this is a New Testament revelation.

Answer: "Thou shalt love thy neighbour as thyself: I am the Lord." Leviticus 19:18.

Question: Then God has not changed. Obedience in all ages is respected in heaven only if it is the outgrowth of a love relationship with God. What about faith? Surely that must be a New Testament teaching alone. Is that true, Habakkuk? What word did the Holy Spirit give you on this vital subject?

Answer: "The just shall live by his faith." Habakkuk 2:4.

Question: Great! Then the picture is clear. God gave the gospel concept to His people from the beginning. But the Hebrews corrupted the gospel by their improper use of the law. And it was against the perversion of the law of God, not the law itself, that Paul fought. That is clear. Tell us, David, in your day how was a man justified?

Answer: "Purge me with hyssop, and I shall be clean: wash me, and I shall be whiter than snow. . . . Hide thy face from my sins, and blot out all mine iniquities. Create in me a clean heart, O God; and renew a right spirit within me. Cast me not away from thy presence; and take not thy holy spirit from me. Restore unto me the joy of thy salvation; and uphold me with thy free spirit." Psalm 51:7-12.

There is no clearer expression of grace anywhere stated. I

therefore conclude that God's plan for saving men has been the same in all ages.

It is clear, gentlemen, from this enlightening discussion, that much of the confusion today concerning the Christian's relationship to God's holy law is avoidable. We need to understand the complex problem confronting Paul in his day. The Jews believed that they were justified by the law. Paul denied this with the truth that we are justified by faith in Christ.

The Jews believed that by obedience to the law they obtained merit with God. Paul denied this. He boldly asserted that merit with God is received of Christ by the believer as an act of grace, a free gift of God. And that obedience to the law is the natural response of the faith-filled believer to the love of God. Marvelous grace! Matchless love!

The ten-commandment law and the prophets span the centuries between the fall of man and the coming of Christ, as God's visible instruments of instruction. As such, they were schoolmasters to bring us to Christ. At this point in time Christ assumed in person this function of the law and prophets and reasserted with clarity their *meaning* and *validity.* He ascended unto God, and the Holy Spirit assumed this function of tutor, pressing home the claims of the law and the prophets to the consciences of men. This plan will reach to the end of the age. The ceremonial law, spanning the centuries until the crucifixion, prefigured Christ's total ministry of salvation for lost men. It told men what Christ would do to save them, and thus brought them to Christ. It was typical in nature, and therefore it was temporary. In no sense is this true of the Ten Commandments.

What Is Jesus Doing Now?

When Jesus returned to heaven He began His work as our great high priest, forgiving our sins when we confess them and enabling us to overcome temptation. We can come boldly to the throne of grace.

14

What Is Jesus Doing Now?

Every act of God for man's salvation is essential and significant. His crucifixion was the supreme revelation of God's love for man. The cross was the focal point of the whole plan of salvation. It is, therefore, central in the great operation of God. It was God's sacrificial atonement for sin. As such, it was adequate and efficacious and within itself complete. In the plan of God, however, the cross was not an isolated event in the saving of man. The cross is meaningful only as it is understood as the focal point of the total operation of God for the saving of man—the Saviour's life, death, resurrection, priestly ministry in heaven, His return to the earth, and the ultimate restoration of the entire universe to a state of sinless beauty.

We will study here the priestly ministry of our Master. Just how is it related to the salvation of man, as indeed it is?

Question: **How truly necessary to man's salvation is the cross?**
Answer: "Without shedding of blood is no remission" of sins. Hebrews 9:22.

Question: **This is true. It was, is, and always will be the blood of Jesus Christ that cleanseth from sin. Paul, was Christ's death alone sufficient to save man?**
Answer: "If Christ be not *raised*, your faith is vain; ye are yet in your sins." 1 Corinthians 15:17.

Question: **Then, Paul, would you say that the cross without the resurrection would not and could not save man?**
Answer: "If Christ be not risen, then is our preaching vain, and your faith is also vain. Yea, and we are found false witnesses of God." 1 Corinthians 15:14, 15.

Question: **Enlightening! Then it seems to me that those who** limit the atoning work of Christ to the cross have a restricted view of the subject. The sacrificial atonement was complete at the cross. But there was still much to be done before man and the entire universe would once more be at one with God. Right, Paul?

Answer: "But for us also, to whom it shall be imputed, if we believe on him that raised up Jesus our Lord from the dead; who was delivered from our offences, and was raised again *for our justification.*" Romans 4:24, 25.

Question: **If Christ were not alive today, the blood that He shed in His death would not avail. Why is this so?**

Answer: "But this man, because he continueth ever, hath an unchangeable priesthood. Wherefore he is able also to save them to the uttermost that come unto God by him, seeing he ever liveth to make intercession for them." Hebrews 7:24, 25.

Question: **I see now why the resurrection is so significant. Unless He were alive He could not intercede for us. We need His intercession. We need His priestly ministry. But why?**

Answer: "Wherefore he is able also to save them to the uttermost." Hebrews 7:25.

Question: **"To the uttermost" includes cleansing us, helping us to overcome sinful habits, and eventually translating us—in other words, justification, sanctification, and translation. Being alive, Jesus is able to administer the benefits of the sacrificial atonement to every seeker. David, how do you understand the blessing of this instant access to a living God?**

Answer: "God is our refuge and strength, a very present help in trouble." Psalm 46:1.

Question: **For whose benefit does Christ serve now as High Priest?**

Answer: "Christ is not entered into the holy places made with hands, which are the figures of the true; but into heaven itself, now to appear in the presence of God for us." Hebrews 9:24.

Question: **John, how necessary to salvation is the present work of Christ?**

Answer: "My little children, these things write I unto you, that ye sin not. And if any man sin, we have an advocate with the Father, Jesus Christ the righteous." 1 John 2:1.

Question: **As our legal Representative in heaven, what merit or**

114

worthiness does Jesus have to offer for us there at the throne?

Answer: "He is the propitiation for our sins: and not for our's only, but also for the sins of the whole world." 1 John 2:2.

Question: **That is clear. We have no merit, so Christ offers His own merit. He is our substitute. This is vital. Why is this so, David?**

Answer: "If thou, Lord, shouldest mark iniquities, O Lord, who shall stand?" Psalm 130:3.

Question: **Since man's best is inadequate, no matter how good, David, were you ever discouraged?**

Answer: "I wait for the Lord, my soul doth wait, and in his word do I hope. My soul waiteth for the Lord more than they that watch for the morning: I say, more than they that watch for the morning." Psalm 130:5, 6.

Question: **So the Lord must cover our best deeds and our most faithful obedience with His blood, His own divine merit. But will He actually do this?**

Answer: "Let Israel hope in the Lord: for with the Lord there is mercy, and with him is plenteous redemption. And he shall redeem Israel from all his iniquities." Psalm 130:7, 8.

Question: **If our best on earth must be covered in heaven by the merit of Christ, then is it necessary to obey at all?**

Answer: "If ye love me, keep my commandments." John 14:15.

Question: **Then we obey Him, not because our deeds are perfect, but because we love Him who is perfect. Paul, how will this love affect us?**

Answer: "The love of Christ constraineth us; because we thus judge, that if one died for all, then were all dead." 2 Corinthians 5:14.

Question: **Then it is love that constrains, or inspires and encourages us to higher levels of conduct. David, do you agree?**

Answer: "Blessed is the man whose strength is in thee; in whose heart are the ways of them. . . . They go from strength to strength, every one of them in Zion appeareth before God." Psalm 84:5-7.

Question: **That is clear. The deeper the love for God, the more perfect our obedience. I accept this. Paul, you have spoken of sub-**

stitution and intercession as the work that Christ is doing now for sinners. What else is He doing?

Answer: "There is one God, and one mediator between God and men, the man Christ Jesus." 1 Timothy 2:5.

Question: **Why does a sinner need a mediator?**

Answer: "But now hath he obtained a more excellent ministry, by how much also he is the mediator of a better covenant, which was established upon better promises." Hebrews 8:6.

Question: **He is the connecting link between God and man in the re-establishment of the agreement between God and man. The new covenant was in fact the original one made in Eden. Adam and Eve broke this agreement. Christ, in taking man's flesh and place, made the terms of the new covenant possible to man and believing man's offering acceptable to God. Paul, how was He thus able to satisfy God?**

Answer: "Such an high priest became us, who is holy, harmless, undefiled, separate from sinners, and made higher than the heavens." Hebrews 7:26.

Question: **Yes, in His divinity, He was all of this. But how could one so exalted succor man?**

Answer: "Seeing then that we have a great high priest, that is passed into the heavens, Jesus the Son of God, let us hold fast our profession. For we have not an high priest which cannot be touched with the feeling of our infirmities; but was in all points tempted like as we are, yet without sin." Hebrews 4:14, 15.

Question: **In His human nature Christ is akin to us and can both sympathize with and succor us. But David, you introduced a new element into the discussion a few minutes ago when you said, "Every one of them in Zion appeareth before God." Paul, what did he mean?**

Answer: "We must all appear before the judgment seat of Christ; that every one may receive the things done in his body, according to that he hath done, whether it be good or bad." 2 Corinthians 5:10.

Question: **Solomon, how searching is this judgment?**

Answer: "God shall bring every work into judgment, with every secret thing, whether it be good, or whether it be evil." Ecclesiastes 12:14.

Question: **Luke, will you comment on the degree of exposure** involved in the judgment?

Answer: "For there is nothing covered, that shall not be revealed; neither hid, that shall not be known. Therefore whatsoever ye have spoken in darkness shall be heard in the light; and that which ye have spoken in the ear in closets shall be proclaimed upon the housetops." Luke 12:2, 3.

Question: **Is there any Bible evidence that an investigation of people's lives will precede the second coming of Christ?**

Answer: "Behold, I come quickly; and my reward is with me, to give every man according as his work shall be." Revelation 22:12.

Question: **Christ clearly states here that when He comes the second time, a decision will already have been made in each case. Is there any other evidence?**

Answer: "There was a tabernacle made; the first, wherein was the candlestick, and the table, and the shewbread; which is called the sanctuary. And after the second veil, the tabernacle which is called the Holiest of all." Hebrews 9:2, 3.

Question: **In the first apartment of the earthly sanctuary, the priest was mediator, intercessor, and substitute. Thus, under Levitical law the priest typified Christ. How often did he officiate in the first apartment of the tabernacle?**

Answer: "Now when these things were thus ordained, the priests went always into the first tabernacle, accomplishing the service of God." Hebrews 9:6.

Question: **In his daily ministry in the first apartment of the sanctuary, with what did the priest secure promise of the sinner's pardon? Moses, can you answer this?**

Answer: "Now this is that which thou shalt offer upon the altar; two lambs of the first year day by day continually." Exodus 29:38.

Question: **We know that the blood of calves, goats, bullocks, doves, and lambs was offered daily for the sins of the people. Why, and how often did the priest go into the Holy of Holies?**

Answer: "Into the second went the high priest alone once every year, not without blood, which he offered for himself, and for the errors of the people." Hebrews 9:7.

Question: **We know that this solemn visit into the Holy of**

Holies occurred on the tenth day of the seventh month each year.
Exodus 16:29. Now in what sense is the word *atonement* ever used
to also mean "cleansing"?

Answer: "For on that day shall the priest make an atonement
for you, to cleanse you, that ye may be clean from all your sins
before the Lord." Leviticus 16:30.

Question: **So the Day of Atonement was a day of judgment and
cleansing. A solemn thought. Why do you mention all of this?**

Answer: That "was a figure for the time then present." Hebrews 9:9.

Question: **A "figure." What do you mean by this?**

Answer: "The law having a shadow of good things to come,
and not the very image of the things." Hebrews 10:1.

Question: **So the earthly tabernacle and its services foresha-
dowed good things that were then future. In a former lesson we
considered that much of the Temple services refers to Christ's
earthly sacrifice as "the Lamb of God." Now we learn that more
was involved. Is that right?**

Answer: "It was therefore necessary that the patterns of
things in the heavens should be purified with these; but the
heavenly things themselves with better sacrifices than these."
Hebrews 9:23.

Question: **That is a shocking statement. Do heavenly things
need purifying? How is this done and by whom?**

Answer: "For then must he often have suffered since the
foundation of the world: but now once in the end of the world
hath he appeared to put away sin by the sacrifice of himself."
Hebrews 9:26.

Question: **Then the putting away of sin in heaven in the last
days by Christ purifies or cleanses the heavenly sanctuary. Marvelous! Now let us listen to Daniel. What did the angel tell you,
Daniel?**

Answer: "He said unto me, Unto two thousand and three
hundred days; then shall the sanctuary be cleansed." Daniel
8:14.

Question: **In Bible prophecy we reckon a day for a year (Ezekiel 4:6). So here we are dealing with 2300 literal years. That is
clear. Daniel, when should we start counting these 2300 years?**

Answer: "Know therefore and understand, that from the going forth of the commandment to restore and to build Jerusalem . . ." Daniel 9:25.

Question: **We know that the executive decree of Artaxerxes went forth in the fall of 457 B.C. Twenty-three hundred years later would bring us to 1844. Daniel, specifically what was to happen then?**

Answer: "The judgment was set, and the books were opened." Daniel 7:10, last part.

Question: **Since the ministry in the earthly sanctuary was a figure of the heavenly, the High Priest in 1844 entered into the Holy of Holies. During His stay there, Daniel, what happened?**

Answer: "I saw in the night visions, and, behold, one like the Son of man came with the clouds of heaven, and came to the Ancient of days, and they brought him near before him. And there was given him dominion and glory, and a kingdom, that all people, nations, and languages, should serve him: his dominion is an everlasting dominion, which shall not pass away, and his kingdom that which shall not be destroyed." Daniel 7:13, 14.

Question: **When the judgment is finished, Daniel, what then will happen?**

Answer: "At that time shall Michael stand up, the great prince which standeth for the children of thy people: and there shall be a time of trouble, such as never was since there was a nation even to that same time: and at that time thy people shall be delivered, every one that shall be found written in the book." Daniel 12:1.

Question: **John, what pronouncement will indicate that Christ's ministry of mercy will then be at an end, and destinies will be forever fixed?**

Answer: "He that is unjust, let him be unjust still: and he which is filthy, let him be filthy still: and he that is righteous, let him be righteous still: and he that is holy, let him be holy still." Revelation 22:11.

This study clearly establishes that Christ is now judging the world prior to His second coming. Our destinies will be fixed when our Lord appears in the clouds. But why does God take the time to investigate the living and the dead? Does He not already know all things? Why then is this necessary? True, God knows all things, but angels and men do not. When all is done, they must acknowledge, "Just and true art thou, thou King of saints." The investigations and records are for the sake of the onlooking universe.

Second, it is for the doomed men and angels. They are self-righteously bold in their rebellion. Only the record of their sins will produce the overwhelming realization of guilt that will force them to their knees. For in that day "every knee shall bow," and every tongue will confess that Jesus Christ is the Lord, to the glory of God the Father. When God at last stands vindicated in His own creation, then only will He unleash His fury against the enemies of His government. Evil men and demons will reap what they sow, but only when they stand exposed for what they are and always were—treacherous rebels against the righteous government of a loving God.

Can the Races Live Together?

All men are equal in the sight of God. Anyone worthy of the name of Christ will honor all men alike, irrespective of race, status, or social position.

15

Can the Races
Live Together?

Racial prejudice is well-nigh universal. In every race and nation this strange attitude persists. Historical and scientific discoveries notwithstanding, men cling to the myth of inherent superiority based on race or national origin. Because of this, the pages of history are dipped in blood, and news media portray the continuing violence. Prejudice is a stubbornly persistent malady and ridiculous when subjected to objective scrutiny.

It is a fact that whatever race or nation has been most powerful at a given time in history has insisted on the mental and cultural inferiority of its less fortunate neighbors. Its scientists have tailor-made their theories to support the myth, and its historians have de-emphasized and sometimes concealed the records of the accomplishments of others to feed the ego of the oppressor. "It just doesn't pay to be down."

Perhaps the cruelest form of racial repression is slavery. It is sheer barbarism, and that alone would lead one race to enslave another. At its worst, laws are passed to guarantee perpetual servitude. The slave is brutalized to convince him of his own worthlessness. The ultimate result is to demean, dehumanize, and debase. There follows the exploitation of man as of an animal for financial gain.

We turn to the prophets for light. These men speak for God. Perhaps in their counsel we shall find surcease from this—the pain of human pride.

Question: **Paul, is it somehow possible that all members of the human family are physically related?**

Answer: God "hath made of one blood all nations of men for to dwell on all the face of the earth, and hath determined the times before appointed, and the bounds of their habitation." Acts 17:26.

Question: **Malachi, Paul has indicated that all men are physically related. This had been proved day after day on the battlefields of the world, by blood transfusions to the wounded. But who is our common father?**

Answer: "Have we not all one father? hath not one God created us? why do we deal treacherously every man against his brother, by profaning the covenant of our fathers?" Malachi 2:10.

Question: **But how did the races get their different languages and become so widely scattered? Moses, do you know?**

Answer: "The Lord came down to see the city and the tower, which the children of men builded. And the Lord said, Behold, the people is one, and they have all one language; and this they begin to do: and now nothing will be restrained from them, which they have imagined to do. Go to, let us go down, and there confound their language, that they may not understand one another's speech. . . . Therefore . . . the Lord did there confound the language of all the earth: and from thence did the Lord scatter them abroad upon the face of all the earth." Genesis 11:5-9.

Question: **Thank you, Moses. You not only answered the question, but you substantiated Paul and Malachi concerning the oneness of the human family, for you quoted the Lord as saying that at that time in human history, "the people is one, and they have all one language." Good. But you know, Moses, that Noah cursed his son Ham for an act of disrespect. Did this in any way affect his color?**

Answer: "He said, Cursed be Canaan; a servant of servants shall he be unto his brethren." Genesis 9:25.

Question: **Why, this does not even mention color. Furthermore, Canaan seems to bear the brunt of this curse, hence the inhabitants of Africa are not here involved. Thanks, Moses, for clearing this up. But is it true that the whole human family descended from Noah?**

Answer: "These are the families of the sons of Noah, after their generations, in their nations: and by these were the nations divided in the earth after the flood." Genesis 10:32.

Question: **In the long history of man, Asia, Africa, Europe, and America have exercised world influence. Red, black, white, and yellow rulers have exercised world power. David, is it because there is some inherent superiority in a race that it predominates at a certain time?**

Answer: "For promotion cometh neither from the east, nor from the west, nor from the south. But God is the judge: he putteth down one, and setteth up another." Psalm 75:6, 7.

Question: **Daniel, Babylon with its brown-skinned people was once a world empire. What did you tell its king at the height of his power?**

Answer: "This matter is by the decree of the watchers, and the demand by the word of the holy ones: to the intent that the living may know that the most High ruleth in the kingdom of men, and giveth it to whomsoever he will, and setteth up over it the basest of men." Daniel 4:17.

Question: **The answer is clear. Often the basest of men gain power over their fellow man. And God is the true power in the earth. Good. But tell us, Paul, is God partial to one race over another?**

Answer: "There is no respect of persons with God." Romans 2:11.

Question: **A good thing to know. But how should our knowledge of this fact affect our behavior one to another, as in an employer-employee situation?**

Answer: "And, ye masters, do the same things unto them, forbearing threatening: knowing that your Master also is in heaven; neither is there respect of persons with him." Ephesians 6:9.

Question: **In view of this, may we expect impartiality in Heaven's administering justice?**

Answer: "He that doeth wrong shall receive for the wrong which he hath done: and there is no respect of persons." Colossians 3:25.

Question: **Ezra, Paul wrote in New Testament times. You tell us, has God always been impartial?**

Answer: "Wherefore now let the fear of the Lord be upon you; take heed and do it: for there is no iniquity with the Lord our God, nor respect of persons, nor taking of gifts." 2 Chronicles 19:7.

Question: **John, what is the sign of Christian discipleship?**
Answer: "By this shall all men know that ye are my disciples, if ye have love one to another." John 13:35.

Question: **But, John, can't I love God without having to love everyone? There are some distasteful characters in this world, you know.**
Answer: "If a man say, I love God, and hateth his brother, he is a liar: for he that loveth not his brother whom he hath seen, how can he love God whom he hath not seen?" 1 John 4:20.

Question: **Clear! But is it necessary? Can I be saved and not do this?**
Answer: "This commandment have we from him, That he who loveth God love his brother also." 1 John 4:21.

Question: **But are all men, even slaves, my brothers? Paul, you returned a slave to his master. What was your counsel?**
Answer: "Perhaps he therefore departed for a season, that thou shouldest receive him for ever; not now as a servant, but above a servant, a brother beloved, specially to me, but how much more unto thee, both in the flesh, and in the Lord?" Philemon 15, 16.

Question: **Only the purest religion could require this of its adherents. But is it possible to love some people while being afraid to fellowship with them?**
Answer: "There is no fear in love; but perfect love casteth out fear: because fear hath torment. He that feareth is not made perfect in love." 1 John 4:18.

Question: **Luke, how did Peter overcome his fear of associating with men of different races?**
Answer: "Then called he them in, and lodged them. And on the morrow Peter went away with them, and certain brethren from Joppa accompanied him. . . . And he said unto them, Ye know how that it is an unlawful thing for a man that is a Jew to keep company, or come unto one of another nation; but God hath shewed me that I should not call any man common or unclean." Acts 10:23-28.

Question: **Clear. But suppose I have an enemy, surely I can at least dislike him. Matthew, what does Jesus say?**

Answer: "But I say unto you, Love your enemies, bless them that curse you, do good to them that hate you, and pray for them which despitefully use you, and persecute you." Matthew 5:44.

Question: **That is very difficult, Matthew. Isn't it much easier to love your friends?**

Answer: "For if ye love them which love you, what reward have ye? do not even the publicans the same? And if ye salute your brethren only, what do ye more than others? do not even the publicans so?" Matthew 5:46, 47.

Question: **But such love is unnatural to human nature. Indeed, is it at all possible to love like God loves? Paul, will you answer, please?**

Answer: "And hope maketh not ashamed; because the love of God is shed abroad in our hearts by the Holy Ghost which is given unto us." Romans 5:5.

Question: **Ah, I knew it would take a miracle, but God will perform it. James, have you a further suggestion?**

Answer: "My brethren, have not the faith of our Lord Jesus Christ, the Lord of glory, with respect of persons. For if there come unto your assembly a man with a gold ring, in goodly apparel, and there come in also a poor man in vile raiment; and ye have respect to him that weareth the gay clothing, and say unto him, Sit thou here in a good place; and say to the poor, Stand thou there, or sit here under my footstool: are ye not then partial in yourselves, and are become judges of evil thoughts? . . . If ye fulfill the royal law according to the scripture, Thou shalt love thy neighbour as thyself, ye do well: but if ye have respect to persons, ye commit sin, and are convinced of the law as transgressors." James 2:1-9.

Well said, James, and thank you, gentlemen, for this enlightening discussion. No question arouses heated emotions like this one. But our Master has said, "And ye shall know the truth, and the truth shall make you free." John 8:32. The truth is often painful, but it is ever helpful. Opinions long cherished are not easily surrendered. Prejudice is an idol whose worship requires its sacrifice in blood.

The wheels of the gods grind slowly, but exceedingly fine.

Ask the Prophets

The slow pendulum of history swings on, and only the thin veil of time separates oppressor and oppressed. Today's master is tomorrow's slave. Such is the lesson of history. But how long must this cycle of misery continue? You can do something about it. Every man can become an island of love in a sea of hate. The inky black darkness of human hate can be dispelled. Some are so discouraged by the forest that they do not fell a single tree. The world awaits the sweet sunrise of human happiness and peace. The song of the angels, "On earth peace, good will toward men," must pass from dream to reality. Wherever you are, *it must, it can,* and by God's grace, *it will!*

Of Capital and Labor

16

Of Capital and Labor

Tensions between employer and employee are mounting. During early years management formulated and executed policy. Business operated without regulation. Children were hired to do men's work for low wages, and men were forced to work for low pay or starve. Government entered the picture, and the working man received some protection. Then labor began to organize. In the beginning it was a violent scene. As the working man met resistance, he fought fire with fire. Ugly stories blight this portion of our history, stories that both management and labor would prefer to forget.

Today labor and management face each other as equals at the negotiating table. What does the Bible say to both? Intransigence on the part of either or both can destroy the nation and imperil the world. Every vital function necessary to human life hangs on the delicate balance of capital-labor relationships. Inspiration has shed some light on this subject. Here follows an "interview" with the prophets on the subject of capital and labor.

Question: **Moses, what indication have we that from the beginning man should labor with his hands?**

Answer: "The Lord God took the man, and put him into the garden of Eden to dress it and to keep it." Genesis 2:15.

Question: **How did the sin of man affect his work program?**

Answer; "Cursed is the ground for thy sake; in sorrow shalt thou eat of it all the days of thy life. . . . In the sweat of thy face shalt thou eat bread, till thou return unto the ground." Genesis 3:17-19.

Question: **Thank you, Moses. Solomon, you are renowned for** your wisdom. What have you to say of the dignity of labor?

Answer: "The labour of the righteous tendeth to life: the fruit of the wicked to sin." Proverbs 10:16.

Question: **Is there an immediate benefit for diligence that would make you recommend it?**

Answer: "He becometh poor that dealeth with a slack hand: but the hand of the diligent maketh rich. He that gathereth in summer is a wise son: but he that sleepeth in harvest is a son that causeth shame." Proverbs 10:4, 5.

Question: **Paul, what do you say of a man who will not support his family?**

Answer: "If any provide not for his own, and specially for those of his own house, he hath denied the faith, and is worse than an infidel." 1 Timothy 5:8.

Question: **What attitude should I take in disputes over money that may tend to violence?**

Answer: "Perverse disputings of men of corrupt minds, and destitute of the truth, supposing that gain is godliness: from such withdraw thyself. But godliness with contentment is great gain." 1 Timothy 6:5, 6.

Question: **Paul, are you saying that it is all right for the rich to oppress the laborer without restraint?**

Answer: "For the scripture saith, Thou shalt not muzzle the ox that treadeth out the corn. And, The labourer is worthy of his reward." 1 Timothy 5:18.

Question: **James, what is God's attitude toward the rich who will not pay a decent wage?**

Answer: "Behold, the hire of the labourers who have reaped down your fields, which is of you kept back by fraud, crieth: and the cries of them which have reaped are entered into the ears of the Lord of sabaoth." James 5:4.

Question: **What curse is pronounced upon rich men who will not mend their ways?**

Answer: "Go to now, ye rich men, weep and howl for your miseries that shall come upon you. Your riches are corrupted, and your garments are motheaten. Your gold and silver is cankered; and the rust of them shall be a witness against you, and shall eat your flesh as it were fire. Ye have heaped treasure together for the last days." James 5:1-3.

Question: **Is it a sin to be rich, Solomon?**
Answer: "For wisdom is a defence, and money is a defence: but the excellency of knowledge is, that wisdom giveth life to them that have it." Ecclesiastes 7:12.

Question: **Paul, is it a sin to have money?**
Answer: "For the love of money is the root of all evil: which while some coveted after, they have erred from the faith, and pierced themselves through with many sorrows." 1 Timothy 6:10.

Question: **Now I understand. It is not a sin to have money. But to love it is wrong. Matthew, how dangerous did Jesus say it is to be rich?**
Answer: "He also that received seed among the thorns is he that heareth the word; and the care of this world, and the deceitfulness of riches, choke the word, and he becometh unfruitful." Matthew 13:22.

Question: **Solomon, is it possible to be rich and spiritually secure?**
Answer: "The blessing of the Lord, it maketh rich, and he addeth no sorrow with it." Proverbs 10:22.

Question: **Moses, what should the rich ever remember?**
Answer: "Thou shalt remember the Lord thy God: for it is he that giveth thee power to get wealth, that he may establish his covenant which he sware unto thy fathers, as it is this day." Deuteronomy 8:18.

From this interview it is clear that a Heaven-regulated relationship between management and labor will result in mutual prosperity. Conversely, either or both pursuing selfish ends can bring only disaster to themselves and society. The will of God must govern all our relationships, or human blindness will destroy us all.

World Peace:
Its Prospects

17

World Peace:
Its Prospects

The sad history of man is largely centered in wars of conquest or repression. Since Cain killed Abel violence has plagued the human family. Wars have become more expensive in money and human lives with the discovery of deadlier weapons. History has glorified her warriors, some of them madmen who swam to power through rivers of blood.

But man has not given up the struggle for peace. The old League of Nations and the United Nations organization are efforts in this direction. However, the performance thus far gives little hope for the future. The League of Nations could not prevent World War II. What then will prevent a third world conflagration? Must man look elsewhere? Here follows an interview with the prophets on this important subject.

Question: **James, why do men fight wars when most people hate violence?**

Answer: "From whence come wars and fightings among you? come they not hence, even of your lusts that war in your members? Ye lust, and have not: ye kill, and desire to have, and cannot obtain: ye fight and war, yet ye have not, because ye ask not." James 4:1, 2.

Question: **Isaiah, do you agree with James?**

Answer: "There is no peace, saith my God, to the wicked." Isaiah 57:21.

Question: **But what about the United Nations? Will it succeed in keeping the peace? Isaiah, have you an answer?**

Answer: "Associate yourselves, O ye people, and ye shall be broken in pieces; and give ear, all ye of far countries: gird yourselves, and ye shall be broken in pieces; gird yourselves, and ye shall be broken in pieces. Take counsel together, and it shall come to nought; speak the word, and it shall not stand: for God is with us." Isaiah 8:9, 10.

Question: **Luke, can you paint a brighter picture? Will not man rise up and renounce the madness of war? What did Jesus say to this?**

Answer: "But when ye shall hear of wars and commotions, be not terrified: for these things must first come to pass; but the end is not by and by. Then said he unto them, Nation shall rise against nation, and kingdom against kingdom." Luke 21:9, 10.

Question: **But man has made spectacular advances in space. Science is in her finest hour. Joel, will this burst of inventive genius make for peace?**

Answer: "Proclaim ye this among the Gentiles; Prepare war, wake up the mighty men, let all the men of war draw near; let them come up: beat your plowshares into swords, and your pruninghooks into spears." Joel 3:9, 10.

Question: **But Joel, you are speaking of the industrial nations, those capable of producing armaments. What of the underdeveloped nations? Will they not exercise a restraining influence?**

Answer: "Let the weak say, I am strong. Assemble yourselves, and come, all ye heathen, and gather yourselves together round about: . . . the heathen be wakened, and come up to the valley of Jehoshaphat." Joel 3:10-12.

Question: **Jonah, what will it take to save the human family now? Nineveh was condemned. What did the king do to save it?**

Answer: "He arose from his throne, and he laid his robe from him, and covered him with sackcloth, and sat in ashes." Jonah 3:6.

Question: **Amazing that the head of a nation should so humble himself before the Lord! But I understand that he did more. Is that right, Jonah?**

Answer: "He caused it to be proclaimed and published through Nineveh by the decree of the king and his nobles, saying, Let neither man nor beast, herd nor flock, taste any thing: let them not feed, nor drink water: but let man and beast be covered with sackcloth, and cry mightily unto God: yea, let them turn every one from his evil way, and from the violence that is in their hands." Jonah 3:7, 8.

Ask the Prophets

Question: **Awe inspiring! The sight of a whole city fasting and in prayer. I notice also that they were to turn from their evil ways. This is the answer for the world. Thank you, Jonah. Just one more question: Did it get results?**

Answer: "God saw their works, that they turned from their evil way; and God repented of the evil, that he had said that he would do unto them; and he did it not." Jonah 3:10.

Question: **Paul, with this example before them, will men today repent and turn from their wicked ways?**

Answer: "This know also, that in the last days perilous times shall come." 2 Timothy 3:1.

Question: **You mention 19 sins that will be universal in our day. Will you name two of the more serious offenses?**

Answer: "Having a form of godliness, but denying the power thereof: from such turn away. For of this sort are they which creep into houses, and lead captive silly women laden with sins, led away with divers lusts." 2 Timothy 3:5, 6.

Question: **Paul, you certainly have described our day. Matthew, how did Jesus describe our day?**

Answer: "As the days of Noe were, so shall also the coming of the Son of man be. For as in the days that were before the flood they were eating and drinking, marrying and giving in marriage, until the day that Noe entered into the ark, and knew not until the flood came, and took them all away; so shall also the coming of the Son of man be." Matthew 24:37-39.

Question: **Matthew, I notice that Jesus twice uses the phrase, "the coming of the Son of man." Does this mean that Jesus will come again to this earth? Did Jesus comment on this?**

Answer: "Therefore be ye also ready: for in such an hour as ye think not the Son of man cometh." Matthew 24:44.

Question: **Paul, man has invented some fearful weapons. He now has the ability to destroy all life on earth. Will man succeed in this? Will there be anyone on earth when the Lord comes?**

Answer: "The Lord himself shall descend from heaven with a shout, with the voice of the archangel, and with the trump of God: and the dead in Christ shall rise first: then we which are alive and remain shall be caught up together with them in the clouds, to meet the Lord in the air: and so shall we ever be with the Lord." 1 Thessalonians 4:16, 17.

Question: **Good! There is hope for us. God will not allow man to destroy all life. He will come back to the earth before this happens. Paul, this gives me great comfort.**

Answer: "Wherefore comfort one another with these words." 1 Thessalonians 4:18.

Gentlemen, thank you for your timely answers to today's problems. You have pointed the way to the future. Your words are like a searchlight in the darkness. The outlook is grim, but the uplook is bright. As we look to man there is little hope for peace. For this we must look to the Prince of Peace.

Emil Ludwig tells the story of a Frenchman who went away from society and lived as a recluse for twenty years. One day he returned to the city. Standing on a corner watching the soldiers march by, he stared in amazement. Touching a bystander, he asked, "Who are these men?" He was told that they were soldiers. "Where are they coming from?" he asked.

"They are coming from peace," came the impatient answer.

"But where are they going?" persisted the hermit.

"They are going to war," came the rejoinder.

"What do they do in war?" asked the hermit.

"Why, they kill each other and destroy property and do other terrible things."

"What do men do in peace?" he asked.

"They love each other and help each other as much as possible."

"But why are they leaving peace where they love each other to go to war where they hate each other?" inquired the hermit.

"Why, you old fool, everybody knows that soldiers leave peace to go to war to get back to peace."

"That seems so unnecessary," said the hermit sadly, "that men should leave peace to go to war to get back to peace. When they are at peace, why don't they stay there?" Receiving no answer, he returned to the forest.

PAINTING BY HARRY ANDERSON   © BY REVIEW AND HERALD

The people of earth will never be at peace with one another until they let the Prince of Peace into their hearts and accept His way of life.

The Dead Are Dead

18

The Dead Are Dead

The subject of death has haunted man since the death of Abel whom his brother Cain slew. The nature of man has long been the subject of the artist's brush, the poet's verse, and the pen of philosopher and sage. World religions have been built on the concept of natural immortality. This is indeed the foundational pillar of spiritualism. Yet others, proclaiming the mortality of man, cite the gloom of the grave as his ultimate destiny. "Eat, drink, and be merry, for tomorrow we die," they chant.

Attila the Hun had himself buried in three caskets—gold, silver, and iron—and commanded that a river be diverted, his body placed on the bottom of the bed, and then the river rerouted to its normal course, in a vain hope of an eternity of seclusion.

But what do the Scriptures teach? God, who made man, certainly knows his nature. Is man mortal or immortal? Is the grave the end or the beginning? Does death liberate or confine? We turn to the prophets for answers. They have done well thus far; I am sure they can help us now.

Question: **What fatherly counsel did God give Adam that indicates He intended man to live forever?**

Answer: "And the Lord God commanded the man, saying, Of every tree of the garden thou mayest freely eat: but of the tree of the knowledge of good and evil, thou shalt not eat of it: for in the day that thou eatest thereof thou shalt surely die." Genesis 2:16, 17.

Question: **Moses, what evidence have we that Eve was fully aware of God's commandment?**

Answer: "The woman said unto the serpent, We may eat of the fruit of the trees of the garden: but of the fruit of the tree which is in the midst of the garden, God hath said, Ye shall not eat of it, neither shall ye touch it, lest ye die." Genesis 3:2, 3.

Question: **It is clear that God wanted man to live forever on condition that he serve God. Disobedience would bring death, they were warned. In view of this warning, Moses, what could possibly tempt man or woman to eat the forbidden fruit? Moses, what did Satan offer?**

Answer: "For God doth know that in the day ye eat thereof, then your eyes shall be opened, and ye shall be as gods, knowing good and evil." Genesis 3:5.

Question: **So Eve became suspicious of God. She felt that He was holding something back from her. She doubted God. Because of this, she sinned. Adam doubted God. He could not conceive that God could give him another Eve. He sinned. Paul, what was the natural consequence?**

Answer: "Wherefore, as by one man sin entered into the world, and death by sin; and so death passed upon all men, for that all have sinned." Romans 5:12.

Question: **What of those who did not sin as Adam did?**

Answer: "Nevertheless death reigned from Adam to Moses, even over them that had not sinned after the similitude of Adam's transgression, who is the figure of him that was to come." Romans 5:14.

Question: **Paul, I think it would be well, just here, to tell us of the grace of God.**

Answer: "For as by one man's disobedience many were made sinners, so by the obedience of one shall many be made righteous." Romans 5:19.

Question: **Who is this, Paul, who so freely gives us of His grace?**

Answer: "For if by one man's offence death reigned by one; much more they which receive abundance of grace and of the gift of righteousness shall reign in life by one, Jesus Christ." Romans 5:17.

Question: **One more question to you, Paul: Did Adam and Eve break the law when they sinned?**

Answer: "Because the law worketh wrath: for where no law is, there is no transgression." Romans 4:15.

Ask the Prophets

Question: **John, do you agree with Paul?**

Answer: "Whosoever committeth sin transgresseth also the law: for sin is the transgression of the law." 1 John 3:4.

Question: **Now that we have examined the reason for death, let us consider the nature of man. Moses, describe for us, please, how God made man.**

Answer: "The Lord God formed man of the dust of the ground, and breathed into his nostrils the breath of life; and man became a living soul." Genesis 2:7.

Question: **The man himself *is* a soul. He does not *have* one, he *is* one. The only element put into man was the breath of life. Moses, that is clear. Now, when a man dies, what leaves him, David?**

Answer: "His breath goeth forth, he returneth to his earth; in that very day his thoughts perish." Psalm 146:4.

Question: **Moses, this breath is sometimes called the "spirit," is it not?**

Answer: "All the while my breath is in me, and the spirit of God is in my nostrils." Job 27:3.

Question: **It is clear that when man dies only the breath leaves the body. Where does the rest of the man go, saint and sinner?**

Answer: "All go unto one place; all are of the dust, and all turn to dust again." Ecclesiastes 3:20.

Question: **Solomon, what is the essential difference between the living and the dead?**

Answer: "For the living know that they shall die: but the dead know not any thing, neither have they any more a reward; for the memory of them is forgotten. Also their love, and their hatred, and their envy, is now perished; neither have they any more a portion for ever in any thing that is done under the sun." Ecclesiastes 9:5, 6.

Question: **Some say that the dead have some advantage over the living in some far-off resting place. Is this true?**

Answer: "A living dog is better than a dead lion." Ecclesiastes 9:4.

Question: **Moses, what did Eliphaz the Temanite have to say about the nature of man?**

Answer: "Shall mortal man be more just than God? shall a

142

man be more pure than his maker?'' Job 4:17.

Question: **So man is mortal; subject to death. He does not have an immortal soul. Do you agree with this, Paul?**

Answer: "Which in his times he shall shew, who is the blessed and only Potentate, the King of kings, and Lord of lords; who only hath immortality, dwelling in the light which no man can approach unto; whom no man hath seen nor can see: to whom be honour and power everlasting.'' 1 Timothy 6:15, 16.

Question: **The idea that man has an immortal soul came from the pagan philosopher Plato. But Plato did not originate the idea. Moses, who did?**

Answer: "The serpent said unto the woman, Ye shall not surely die.'' Genesis 3:4.

Question: **So the dead are not actually dead, according to the devil. Ezekiel, what does God say?**

Answer: "Behold, all souls are mine; as the soul of the father, so also the soul of the son is mine: but the soul that sinneth, it shall die.'' Ezekiel 18:4.

Question: **So, the soul dies when the man dies. An important point. Paul, how many souls have sinned?**

Answer: "For all have sinned, and come short of the glory of God.'' Romans 3:23.

Question: **John, are human beings the only "souls"?**

Answer: "The second angel poured out his vial upon the sea; and it became as the blood of a dead man: and every living soul died in the sea.'' Revelation 16:3.

Question: **Then even the sea animals are "souls." That is clear. Now, Solomon, does man have any pre-eminence over animals in death?**

Answer: "That which befalleth the sons of men befalleth beasts; even one thing befalleth them: as the one dieth, so dieth the other; yea, they have all one breath; so that a man hath no pre-eminence above a beast: for all is vanity. All go unto one place; all are of the dust, and all turn to dust again.'' Ecclesiastes 3:19, 20.

Question: **Moses, how completely dead are the dead?**

Answer: "As the cloud is consumed and vanisheth away: so he that goeth down to the grave shall come up no more.'' Job 7:9.

Question: **Are you saying, Moses, that the dead have no power to move around? Doesn't some part of the dead return to haunt houses?**

Answer: "He shall return no more to his house, neither shall his place know him any more." Job 7:10.

Question: **When death strikes, where do both the righteous and the wicked go?**

Answer: "They shall go down to the bars of the pit, when our rest together is in the dust." Job 17:16.

Question: **Who is it that appears after death to imitate the dead, John?**

Answer: "For they are the spirits of devils, working miracles, which go forth unto the kings of the earth and of the whole world, to gather them to the battle of that great day of God Almighty." Revelation 16:14.

Question: **Spirits of devils! So they are the culprits. Paul, can they actually change their appearance so as to look like our departed relatives and talk like them? Can they imitate the righteous?**

Answer: "And no marvel; for Satan himself is transformed into an angel of light." 2 Corinthians 11:14.

Question: **If these demons can imitate good angels, then it is easy for them to imitate us. Paul, do you agree?**

Answer: "Therefore it is no great thing if his ministers also be transformed as the ministers of righteousness; whose end shall be according to their works." 2 Corinthians 11:15.

Question: **But why would they do this, John?**

Answer: "The great dragon was cast out, that old serpent, called the devil, and Satan, which deceiveth the whole world: he was cast out into the earth, and his angels were cast out with him." Revelation 12:9.

Question: **They wished to deceive the world. That is clear. He was the original liar, wasn't he, John?**

Answer: "He was a murderer from the beginning, and abode not in the truth, because there is no truth in him. When he speaketh a lie, he speaketh of his own: for he is a liar, and the father of it." John 8:44.

Question: **It was the devil, then, who first said that the dead**

144

are not dead, that some immortal part of man lives on after death. By impersonating the dead, he hopes to perpetuate his lie. Sad to say, he has succeeded too well. Paul, since man is mortal, subject to death, how may we seek immortality?

Answer: "To them who by patient continuance in well doing seek for glory and honour and immortality, eternal life." Romans 2:7.

Question: We must seek this now while we are alive. Why, Solomon?

Answer: "Whatsoever thy hand findeth to do, do it with thy might; for there is no work, nor device, nor knowledge, nor wisdom, in the grave, whither thou goest." Ecclesiastes 9:10.

Question: Good! We qualify for immortality this side of the grave, by obeying the gospel. Then we must wait for it in the grave. Is this not correct, Moses? What did Job say?

Answer: "If a man die, shall he live again? all the days of my appointed time will I wait, till my change come." Job 14:14.

Question: Moses, how did Job describe death?

Answer: "He cometh forth like a flower, and is cut down: he fleeth also as a shadow, and continueth not." Job 14:2.

Question: The devil says that in death a part of man continues to live. God says he *continueth not*. Take your pick. Luke, how did Jesus describe death?

Answer: "All wept, and bewailed her: but he said, Weep not; she is not dead, but sleepeth." Luke 8:52.

Question: Jesus repeated this definition of death at the tomb of Lazarus. Man is unconscious in sleep. He is therefore unconscious in death and will remain so until the last days. Is this so, Moses? What does Job say?

Answer: "I know that my redeemer liveth, and that he shall stand at the latter day upon the earth: and though after my skin worms destroy this body, yet in my flesh shall I see God: whom I shall see for myself, and mine eyes shall behold, and not another." Job 19:25-27.

Question: Job said that the dead would not come up from the grave, meaning under their own power. Let us ask him how they will come up, as obviously they will.

Answer: "Thou shalt call, and I will answer thee: thou wilt have a desire to the work of thine hands.'' Job 14:15.

Question: **John, who is this that will call the dead from their graves? What did Jesus say?**
Answer: ''Verily, verily, I say unto you, The hour is coming, and now is, when the dead shall hear the voice of the Son of God: and they that hear shall live.'' John 5:25.

Question: **John, we know that all the dead will be raised eventually, but the phrase, ''they that hear shall live,'' indicates that not all will be called at the same time. Paul, is this true?**
Answer: ''For the Lord himself shall descend from heaven with a shout, with the voice of the archangel, and with the trump of God: and the dead in Christ shall rise first.'' 1 Thessalonians 4:16.

Question: **So Christians will enjoy the privilege of emerging from the grave first. Paul, what change will take place in their natures at this time?**
Answer: ''For this corruptible must put on incorruption, and this mortal must put on immortality.'' 1 Corinthians 15:53.

Question: **Paul, have you any further comment?**
Answer: ''For our conversation is in heaven; from whence also we look for the Saviour, the Lord Jesus Christ: who shall change our vile body, that it may be fashioned like unto his glorious body, according to the working whereby he is able even to subdue all things unto himself.'' Philippians 3:20, 21.

Question: **By what model shall we then be fashioned?**
Answer: ''Beloved, now are we the sons of God, and it doth not yet appear what we shall be: but we know that, when he shall appear, we shall be like him; for we shall see him as he is.'' 1 John 3:2.

Question: **Thank you, John. It is at this point in time that we will receive immortality. We do not have it now. Paul, how many must sleep the sleep of death?**
Answer: ''And as it is appointed unto men once to die, but after this the judgment.'' Hebrews 9:27.

Question: **Are there any exceptions to this, Paul?**
Answer: ''Behold, I shew you a mystery; We shall not all sleep, but we shall all be changed.'' 1 Corinthians 15:51.

146

Question: **Who are these who will escape death?**

Answer: "For the Lord himself shall descend from heaven with a shout, with the voice of the archangel, and with the trump of God: and the dead in Christ shall rise first: then we which are alive and remain shall be caught up together with them in the clouds, to meet the Lord in the air: and so shall we ever be with the Lord." 1 Thessalonians 4:16, 17.

Question: **Those righteous who are alive will be changed and translated without seeing death. Clear. John, what is the advantage of being in the first resurrection?**

Answer: "Blessed and holy is he that hath part in the first resurrection: on such the second death hath no power, but they shall be priests of God and of Christ, and shall reign with him a thousand years." Revelation 20:6.

Question: **Wonderful. But what of the wicked dead? How much time will pass after the resurrection of the righteous until the resurrection of the wicked?**

Answer: "The rest of the dead lived not again until the thousand years were finished. This is the first resurrection." Revelation 20:5.

Question: **Thank you, John. There will be a thousand-year period between the first and second resurrection. Paul, what is the last enemy to be destroyed?**

Answer: "The last enemy that shall be destroyed is death." 1 Corinthians 15:26.

Thank you, gentlemen. Death has been proclaimed as a friend ushering us into the very presence of the Lord. Now we know better. Death is an enemy. It is cessation of life. It is sleep, an unconscious state. It is the wages of sin, not the gift of God. Though we hate to face it, the gospel of the Lord Jesus enables us to die in peace. "Yea, though I walk through the valley of the shadow of death, I will fear no evil: for thou art with me; thy rod and thy staff they comfort me." Psalm 23:4. Add to this the glorious hope of life in endless eternity after the resurrection, and you have a hope that makes death bearable. "Comfort one another with these words," said the apostle. It is the author's prayer that these words have done just that for you.

When Christ appears in the clouds of heaven at the last day, the wicked will pray to the rocks and the mountains to fall on them and hide them from His presence.

The Lord's Day

19

The Lord's Day

The Lord's day is a day special unto Himself. He has chosen, however, to share this blessing with man. Our obligation to keep the Sabbath receives its force not from legal sanction (though indeed it does have legal sanction) but from the Lord Himself, the Author and Executor of all divine law. While rebellious man through the centuries has debated and resisted the claims of God's special day, believers have found in it a source of weekly spiritual refreshment. We shall ask the prophets to identify the day, and to explain God's purpose in setting it aside as a holy day.

Question: **John, we know that God set aside a special day of the week for His believers to observe. What was your attitude on that day?**

Answer: "I was in the Spirit on the Lord's day, and heard behind me a great voice, as of a trumpet." Revelation 1:10.

Question: **Isaiah, in Old Testament times did God claim a special day as His?**

Answer: "If thou turn away thy foot from the sabbath, from doing thy pleasure on my holy day; and call the sabbath a delight, the holy of the Lord, honourable; and shalt honour him, not doing thine own ways, nor finding thine own pleasure, nor speaking thine own words: then shalt thou delight thyself in the Lord." Isaiah 58:13, 14.

Question: **Isaiah, you have helped us. You speak of the Sabbath and the Lord's day as one and the same. An important clue. Now, Moses, which day did God claim as His day in the law?**

Answer: "The seventh day is the sabbath of the Lord thy God." Exodus 20:10.

Question: **Moses, was the seventh day sacred in Eden?**

Answer: "On the seventh day God ended his work which he had made; and he rested on the seventh day from all his work which he had made. And God blessed the seventh day, and sanctified it: because that in it he had rested from all his work which God created and made." Genesis 2:2, 3.

Question: **But how may we know that the seventh day of Creation is the seventh day today?**

Answer: "I know that, whatsoever God doeth, it shall be for ever: nothing can be put to it, nor any thing taken from it: and God doeth it, that men should fear before him. That which hath been is now; and that which is to be hath already been; and God requireth that which is past." Ecclesiastes 3:14, 15.

Question: **So nothing has changed the day. Interestingly enough men who are authoritative in this field agree. At Creation there were seven days to the week. Today there are seven; the same seven. Mark, would you agree that the seventh day of the week today is the same as it was at Creation?**

Answer: "The even was come, because it was the preparation, that is, the day before the sabbath." Mark 15:42.

Question: **This was the weekly preparation day and therefore the day we call "good Friday." Mark, you called it "the day before the sabbath." That makes *Saturday* the Sabbath or Lord's day. If, then, the day of the crucifixion is the day before the Sabbath or Lord's day, how is the day that follows the Sabbath designated?**

Answer: "When the sabbath was past, Mary Magdalene, and Mary the mother of James, and Salome, had bought sweet spices, that they might come and anoint him. And very early in the morning the first day of the week, they came unto the sepulchre at the rising of the sun." Mark 16:1, 2.

Question: **You are clear on two things here, Mark: (1) Sunday cannot be the Lord's day, or Sabbath, for the Lord's day was *past* when Sunday came; (2) the Lord's day is the day after Friday. Only one day stands between Friday and Sunday and that is *Saturday.* Hence, it is the Lord's day and the same seventh day as at Creation. Luke, do you agree with Mark?**

Answer: "That day was the preparation, and the sabbath drew on." Luke 23:54.

Question: **So you do agree with Mark that the day of the crucifixion is the day before the Lord's day. Now what did the people do on the Sabbath?**

Answer: "They returned, and prepared spices and ointments; and rested the sabbath day according to the commandment." Luke 23:56.

Question: **So the Sabbath commandment was not nailed to the cross, for those closest to Jesus observed it the day after the crucifixion. Now, Mark, on what day did Jesus rise from the grave?**

Answer: "Now when Jesus was risen early the first day of the week, he appeared first to Mary Magdalene, out of whom he had cast seven devils." Mark 16:9.

Question: **Matthew, which day is the Sabbath?**

Answer: "In the end of the sabbath, as it began to dawn toward the first day of the week, came Mary Magdalene and the other Mary to see the sepulchre." Matthew 28:1.

Question: **Prophets of God, is there any place in the Bible, any authority, that says we should observe Sunday as sacred in honor of the resurrection?**

Answer: Silence.

Question: **Do any of you prophets in any of your writings refer to Sunday as the "Lord's day"?**

Answer: Silence.

Question: **Spokesmen of the Most High God, has God revealed to any of you that Friday should be kept holy in honor of the crucifixion?**

Answer: Silence.

Question: **Paul, what ordinance did Jesus give to commemorate His death?**

Answer: "When he had given thanks, he brake it, and said, Take, eat: this is my body, which is broken for you: this do in remembrance of me. After the same manner also he took the cup, when he had supped, saying, This cup is the new testament in my blood: this do ye, as oft as ye drink it, in remembrance of me." 1 Corinthians 11:24, 25.

Question: **How are we to commemorate the resurrection?**

Answer: "Therefore we are buried with him by baptism into death: that like as Christ was raised up from the dead by the glory of the Father, even so we also should walk in newness of life." Romans 6:4.

Question: **So we do not observe Sunday in honor of the resurrection, nor Friday for the crucifixion. But Saturday is to be kept holy in honor of Creation. Moses, isn't that what God said?**

Answer: "Remember the sabbath day, to keep it holy. . . . For in six days the Lord made heaven and earth, the sea, and all that in them is, and rested the seventh day: wherefore the Lord blessed the sabbath day, and hallowed it." Exodus 20:8-11.

Question: **So the Sabbath is a weekly reminder to man of his own and the world's creation. Were it faithfully observed the world around, there would be no evolutionists. Tell us, David, is the Sabbath as important as the other things God has commanded?**

Answer: "The works of his hands are verity and judgment; all his commandments are sure. They stand fast for ever and ever, and are done in truth and uprightness." Psalm 111:7, 8.

Question: **When does the Sabbath begin and end, Moses?**

Answer: "It shall be unto you a sabbath of rest, and ye shall afflict your souls; in the ninth day of the month at even, from even unto even, shall ye celebrate your sabbath." Leviticus 23:32.

Question: **Mark, we know that the sunset varies in time with the seasons, but how may we know when the even comes?**

Answer: "And at even, when the sun did set, they brought unto him all that were diseased, and them that were possessed with devils." Mark 1:32.

Question: **Moses, if I cannot get permission to be off my job, will God excuse my Sabbath work?**

Answer: "Six days shalt thou labour, and do all thy work: but the seventh day is the sabbath of the Lord thy God: in it thou shalt not do any work." Exodus 20:9, 10.

Question: **But does God expect a man to starve? Isaiah, have you an answer?**

Answer: "If thou turn away thy foot from the sabbath, from doing thy pleasure on my holy day; and call the sabbath a delight, the holy of the Lord, honourable; and shalt honour him, not doing thine own ways, nor finding thine own pleasure, nor speaking thine own words: then shalt thou delight thyself in the Lord; and I will cause thee to ride upon the high places of the earth, and feed thee with the heritage of Jacob thy father: for the mouth of the Lord hath spoken it." Isaiah 58:13, 14.

Question: **Daniel, why do so many people go to church on Sunday? Did someone try to change the law?**

Answer: "He shall speak great words against the most High, and shall wear out the saints of the most High, and think to change times and laws." Daniel 7:25.

Question: **History points an accusing finger at Rome for tampering with God's law and forcing Sunday upon the world. Isaiah, will the true Sabbath survive?**

Answer: "It shall come to pass, that from one new moon to another, and from one sabbath to another, shall all flesh come to worship before me, saith the Lord." Isaiah 66:23.

Question: **So the Sabbath will be kept in the new earth. Very well. But it is said that New Testament Christians kept Sunday. Is this true, Luke?**

Answer: "Paul, as his manner was, went in unto them, and three sabbath days reasoned with them out of the scriptures." Acts 17:2.

Question: **But didn't Paul go to the synagogue just to catch the Jews who worshiped on Saturday?**

Answer: "When the Jews were gone out of the synagogue, the Gentiles besought that these words might be preached to them the next sabbath." Acts 13:42.

Question: **So this was not just a Jewish gathering. There were Gentiles also worshiping on Sabbath. Tell us how the next Sabbath's meeting turned out, Luke.**

Answer: "The next sabbath day came almost the whole city together to hear the word of God." Acts 13:44.

Question: **Great! Jews and Gentiles keeping God's holy day! Now tell us, Luke, did Paul observe the Sabbath thus each week?**

Answer: "He reasoned in the synagogue every sabbath, and persuaded the Jews and the Greeks." Acts 18:4.

Question: **What day did Jesus observe while on earth? Luke, have you an answer?**

Answer: "He came to Nazareth, where he had been brought

154

up: and, as his custom was, he went into the synagogue on the sabbath day, and stood up for to read.'' Luke 4:16.

Question: **So His custom was to keep the Sabbath, not Sunday. But have you another such instance?**

Answer: "But he passing through the midst of them went his way, and came down to Capernaum, a city of Galilee, and taught them on the sabbath days.'' Luke 4:30, 31.

Question: **Some say that every time Christ appeared to the disciples after the resurrection it was on Sunday. There is no proof for this. But if it were true, John, tell us how five of the disciples spent Sunday.**

Answer: "Simon Peter saith unto them, I go a fishing. They say unto him, We also go with thee. They went forth, and entered into a ship immediately; and that night they caught nothing. But when the morning was now come, Jesus stood on the shore.'' John 21:3, 4.

Question: **So, they went fishing that day. Isaiah, what is the reward of the truly faithful?**

Answer: "Blessed is the man that doeth this, and the son of man that layeth hold on it; that keepeth the sabbath from polluting it, and keepeth his hand from doing any evil. . . . Even unto them will I give in mine house and within my walls a place and a name better than of sons and of daughters: I will give them an everlasting name, that shall not be cut off.'' Isaiah 56:2-5.

Thank you, gentlemen. This has been an enlightening discussion. The world must yet learn the importance that God attaches to His holy day. "Moreover also I gave them my sabbaths, to be a sign between me and them, that they might know that I am the Lord that sanctify them.'' "And hallow my sabbaths; and they shall be a sign between me and you, that ye may know that I am the Lord your God.'' Ezekiel 20:12, 20. Such deep meaning must not be ignored by the Christ-loving seeker for truth. Let us all "remember the sabbath day, to keep it holy.''

We are what we eat and drink. Health, happiness, and success in life require that we treat our bodies with at least as much respect as we would a
new automobile. Health is worth more than wealth.

Your Good Health

20

Your Good Health

Man is an integral being. His spiritual, mental, and physical faculties are inseparably interrelated. One cannot suffer or prosper without affecting the others. Little emphasis has been given the subject of physical health by the religious establishment, especially in the realm of diet and habit. The spiritual has taken precedence, to the neglect of the broad health counsel of the Scriptures. Some have made bold to declare the health laws of the Bible as being applicable only to the Jews and therefore not applicable to the Gentiles. What is the truth of the matter? For answers we turn to the prophets of God, for if there is light on the subject they will have it.

Question: **John, in your letter to Gaius, what did you mention praying for?**
Answer: "Beloved, I wish above all things that thou mayest prosper and be in health, even as thy soul prospereth." 3 John 2.

Question: **Paul, what was your burden in this matter?**
Answer: "I beseech you therefore, brethren, by the mercies of God, that ye present your bodies a living sacrifice, holy, acceptable unto God, which is your reasonable service." Romans 12:1.

Question: **Are you saying, Paul, that God is interested in our personal habits?**
Answer: "Whether therefore ye eat, or drink, or whatsoever ye do, do all to the glory of God." 1 Corinthians 10:31.

Question: **We know that "the kingdom of heaven is not meat and drink," but, Paul, just how important is this matter of health**

158

habits? Why must we treat our bodies properly?

Answer: "What? know ye not that your body is the temple of the Holy Ghost which is in you, which ye have of God, and ye are not your own? For ye are bought with a price: therefore glorify God in your body, and in your spirit, which are God's." 1 Corinthians 6:19, 20.

Question: **Luke, what did Peter say in a vision that indicates his eating habits?**

Answer: "Peter said, Not so, Lord; for I have never eaten any thing that is common or unclean." Acts 10:14.

Question: **Of course, we know that the animals on the sheet of this vision represent people (Acts 10:28), but this does tell us of Peter's practice. Paul, what further word from the Lord have you concerning this?**

Answer: "Wherefore come out from among them, and be ye separate, saith the Lord, and touch not the unclean thing; and I will receive you." 2 Corinthians 6:17.

Question: **John, we are about to consult Moses about unclean foods. Can you first tell us if Jesus ever endorsed Moses' writings?**

Answer: "For had ye believed Moses, ye would have believed me: for he wrote of me. But if ye believe not his writings, how shall ye believe my words?" John 5:46, 47.

Question: **Thank you, John. With this endorsement of Jesus, we turn to Moses. In the days of Noah, how were the animals classified with reference to eating?**

Answer: "Of every clean beast thou shalt take to thee by sevens, the male and his female: of beasts that are not clean by two, the male and his female. Of fowls also of the air by sevens, the male and female; to keep seed alive upon the face of all the earth." Genesis 7:2, 3.

Question: **Now we know that the floodwaters destroyed all vegetation, consequently God was going to permit man to eat the flesh of animals in order to stay alive. Moses, what was the diet in Eden for both man and beast?**

Answer: "God said, Behold, I have given you every herb bearing seed, which is upon the face of all the earth, and every tree, in the which is the fruit of a tree yielding seed; to you it shall be for meat. And to every beast of the earth, and to every fowl of the air, and to every thing that creepeth upon the earth, wherein there is life, I have given every green herb for meat: and it was so.'' Genesis 1:29, 30.

Question: **It is interesting that before man sinned no flesh was eaten in the whole animal kingdom. How sin has changed the nature of things! What dietary safeguards did God reveal, for the purpose of good health?**

Answer: "Whatsoever parteth the hoof, and is clovenfooted, and cheweth the cud, among the beasts, that shall ye eat.'' Leviticus 11:3.

Question: **The reader may read the rest of the chapter for details, but what very popular animal is expressly forbidden, and by** *name?*

Answer: "The swine, though he divide the hoof, and be clovenfooted, yet he cheweth not the cud; he is unclean to you. Of their flesh shall ye not eat, and their carcase shall ye not touch; they are unclean to you.'' Leviticus 11:7, 8.

Question: **Moses, in the book of Deuteronomy you repeat this prohibition, don't you?**

Answer: "The swine, because it divideth the hoof, yet cheweth not the cud, it is unclean unto you: ye shall not eat of their flesh, nor touch their dead carcase.'' Deuteronomy 14:8.

Question: **Isaiah, how does God regard those who persist in eating unclean things?**

Answer: "I have spread out my hands . . . unto a rebellious people . . . which eat swine's flesh, and broth of abominable things is in their vessels. . . . These are a smoke in my nose, a fire that burneth all the day.'' Isaiah 65:2-5.

Question: **Will God overlook these sins, Isaiah?**

Answer: "Behold, it is written before me: I will not keep silence, but will recompense, even recompense into their bosom.'' Isaiah 65:6.

Question: **What and when will judgment fall on those who debase their God-given physical powers with their appetites?**

Answer: "Behold, the Lord will come with fire, and with his chariots like a whirlwind, to render his anger with fury, and his rebuke with flames of fire. . . . They that sanctify themselves, and purify themselves in the gardens behind one tree in the midst, eating swine's flesh, and the abomination, and the mouse, shall be consumed together, saith the Lord.'' Isaiah 66:15-17.

Question: **This punishment will come when all other sinners receive their reward, at the end of the world. That is clear. Isaiah, how thorough will the Lord's work be in that day?**

Answer: "For by fire and by his sword will the Lord plead with all flesh: and the slain of the Lord shall be many." Isaiah 66:16.

Question: **Matthew, did not Jesus single out the sin of gluttony as a cause of divine disfavor in Noah's day?**

Answer: "In the days that were before the flood they were eating and drinking, marrying and giving in marriage, until the day that Noe entered into the ark." Matthew 24:38.

Question: **What happened to them?**

Answer: They "knew not until the flood came, and took them all away; so shall also the coming of the Son of man be." Matthew 24:39.

Question: **Matthew, you mentioned drinking. That is a sensitive spot. The drinking of intoxicating and harmful beverages is now socially acceptable. Some men drink as freely as they breathe. Solomon, should men drink intoxicating liquor at all?**

Answer: "Look not thou upon the wine when it is red, when it giveth his colour in the cup, when it moveth itself aright. At the last it biteth like a serpent, and stingeth like an adder." Proverbs 23:31, 32.

Question: **This is prohibition! Don't even look at it, let alone drink it. Good! Am I right in this conclusion?**

Answer: "Wine is a mocker, strong drink is raging: and whosoever is deceived thereby is not wise." Proverbs 20:1.

Question: **This is true. Strong drink is a killer. It also debases the morals. It turns decent fathers into maniacs. Oh, the misery and death that intoxicating liquors have caused. Solomon, tell us about it.**

Answer: "Who hath woe? who hath sorrow? who hath contentions? who hath babbling? who hath wounds without cause? who hath redness of eyes? They that tarry long at the wine; they that go to seek mixed wine." Proverbs 23:29, 30.

Question: **What is the cause of some men's fall?**

Answer: "Yea also, because he transgresseth by wine, he is a proud man, neither keepeth at home, who enlargeth his desire as hell, and is as death, and cannot be satisfied, but gathereth unto him all nations, and heapeth unto him all people." Habakkuk 2:5.

Question: **We know from history that this is true. When the Medes and Persians entered Babylon, the guards were drunk, and the king was in the midst of a drunken orgy. Moses, what instruction did the Lord give the priests that may help us?**

Answer: "Do not drink wine nor strong drink, thou, nor thy sons with thee, when ye go into the tabernacle of the congregation, lest ye die: . . . that ye may put difference between holy and unholy, and between unclean and clean." Leviticus 10:9, 10.

Question: **So it is true that drink interferes with judgment. Luke, what about John the Baptist?**

Answer: "He shall be great in the sight of the Lord, and shall drink neither wine nor strong drink; and he shall be filled with the Holy Ghost, even from his mother's womb." Luke 1:15.

Question: **Can it be that the great in God's sight don't drink intoxicants, nor do those who are filled with the Holy Ghost? An interesting question. Solomon, why is it suggested that kings abstain from drink?**

Answer: "It is not for kings, O Lemuel, it is not for kings to drink wine; nor for princes strong drink: lest they drink, and forget the law, and pervert the judgment of any of the afflicted." Proverbs 31:4, 5.

Question: **Isaiah, how smart are those who drink?**

Answer: "Woe unto them that rise up early in the morning, that they may follow strong drink; that continue until night, till wine inflame them!" Isaiah 5:11.

Question: **What if a man drinks just a little?**

Answer: "Woe unto them that are mighty to drink wine, and men of strength to mingle strong drink." Isaiah 5:22.

Question: **Isaiah, how does strong drink affect the priest and prophet?**

Answer: "They also have erred through wine, and through strong drink are out of the way; the priest and the prophet have erred through strong drink, they are swallowed up of wine, they are out of the way through strong drink; they err in vision, they stumble in judgment." Isaiah 28:7.

Question: If that happens to priests, what about the poor people? Joel, in your call to lamentation you singled out this habit, did you not?

Answer: "Awake, ye drunkards, and weep; and howl, all ye drinkers of wine, because of the new wine; for it is cut off from your mouth." Joel 1:5.

Question: Peter, with what other sins do you class strong drink?

Answer: "The time past of our life may suffice us to have wrought the will of the Gentiles, when we walked in lasciviousness, lusts, excess of wine, revellings, banquetings, and abominable idolatries." 1 Peter 4:3.

Question: That says "excess of wine." Does not this allow moderate drinking?

Answer: "Wherein they think it strange that ye run not with them to the same excess of riot, speaking evil of you." 1 Peter 4:4.

Question: That's clear. If "excess of riot" allows moderate rioting, then "excess of wine" allows moderate drinking. The fact is: Neither is allowed. Paul, wine when drunk tends to excess, does it not?

Answer: "Be not drunk with wine, wherein is excess; but be filled with the Spirit." Ephesians 5:18.

Question: Paul, clear this up for us: Will drinkers of strong drink enter heaven?

Answer: "Envyings, murders, drunkenness, revellings, and such like: of the which I tell you before, as I have also told you in time past, that they which do such things shall not inherit the kingdom of God." Galatians 5:21.

Question: Wine, whisky, beer, and coffee damage the nervous system, the heart, and alimentary tract. Just as seriously they deceive the brain. Moses, what about tobacco, dope, and the various forms of narcotics?

Answer: "Lest there should be among you a root that beareth gall and wormwood [poison herb]; . . . the Lord will not spare him, but then the anger of the Lord and his jealousy shall smoke against that man, and all the curses that are written in this book shall lie upon him, and the Lord shall blot out his name from under heaven." Deuteronomy 29:18-20.

Question: **What about the bartender?**

Answer: "Woe unto him that giveth his neighbour drink, that puttest thy bottle to him, and makest him drunken also, that thou mayest look on their nakedness!" Habakkuk 2:15.

Thank you, gentlemen. The issues are clear. To defile our bodies is to dishonor God and ourselves. The Master has said, "Thou shalt love thy neighbour as thyself." But what if we do not love ourselves enough to bridle our appetites? How then are we capable of loving others? What we take into our bodies affects our attitudes. A diseased body is of little help to the mind. And to willfully maim our bodies is to jeopardize our spiritual attitudes and mental posture. "Ye shall know the truth, and the truth shall make you free." John 8:32.

The Day of the Lord

21

The Day of the Lord

Since the advent of sin, a day of reckoning has been determined. The great controversy between Christ and Satan must be terminated, but it can only end in victory for one and defeat for the other. The universe is too small for two gods. God, to be God, must be Lord of all if Lord at all. The struggle that began in heaven has raged for some 6,000 years on the earth. It cannot go on forever, nor will it. Long ere this the conflict has involved men and angels. Neither needed to become involved. Today Satan has such a strong following on this planet that he is the acknowledged "god of this world." He stakes his claim on the fact of Adam's transgression and the allegiance paid him by the majority of earth's billons of inhabitants. But he is a usurper. "If I were hungry, I would not tell thee: for the world is mine, and the fulness thereof." Psalm 50:12.

But what of the outcome of this conflict? We turn to the prophets for answers, for they alone possess the light we seek.

Question: **Amos, is it true that you prophets have insights the rest of us don't have concerning the future?**

Answer: "Surely the Lord God will do nothing, but he revealeth his secret unto his servants the prophets." Amos 3:7.

Question: **Daniel, what was the source of your unusual wisdom?**

Answer: "But there is a God in heaven that revealeth secrets." Daniel 2:28.

Question: **Peter, are you prophets at liberty to alter your prophecies?**

Answer: "Knowing this first, that no prophecy of the scripture is of any private interpretation." 2 Peter 1:20.

166

Question: **Then we may be sure of what you prophets say? Can we trust you?**

Answer: "We have also a more sure word of prophecy; whereunto ye do well that ye take heed, as unto a light that shineth in a dark place, until the day dawn, and the day star arise in your hearts." 2 Peter 1:19.

Question: **David, why must the Lord *soon* interfere with this cycle of sin and human misery?**

Answer: "It is time for thee, Lord, to work: for they have made void thy law." Psalm 119:126.

Question: **What is the basis of God's claim of world ownership? Isaiah, can you answer?**

Answer: "I have made the earth, and created man upon it: I, even my hands, have stretched out the heavens, and all their host have I commanded." Isaiah 45:12.

Question: **In view of this, what legitimate appeal does the Lord make to earth's inhabitants?**

Answer: "Look unto me, and be ye saved, all the ends of the earth: for I am God, and there is none else." Isaiah 45:22.

Question: **What counterclaim does the devil make?**

Answer: "I will ascend above the heights of the clouds; I will be like the most High." Isaiah 14:14.

Question: **Isaiah, how does God answer him?**

Answer: "Yet thou shalt be brought down to hell, to the sides of the pit." Isaiah 14:15.

Question: **By what method is Lucifer securing followers as he marshals for the final conflict?**

Answer: "The great dragon was cast out, that old serpent, called the Devil, and Satan, which deceiveth the whole world." Revelation 12:9.

Question: **So it is by deception that Satan lures the unwary. John, you mention that Satan was cast out. Please tell us from where he was cast out.**

Answer: "There was war in heaven: Michael and his angels fought against the dragon; and the dragon fought and his angels, and prevailed not; neither was their place found any more in heaven." Revelation 12:7, 8.

Question: **John, what was Lucifer's problem there?**

Answer: "I heard a loud voice saying in heaven, Now is come salvation, and strength, and the kingdom of our God, and the power of his Christ: for the accuser of our brethren is cast down, which accused them before our God day and night." Revelation 12:10.

Question: **So he kept busy day and night spreading dissension. God could not tolerate this forever. Luke, how did Jesus describe Satan's descent from heaven?**

Answer: "And he said unto them, I beheld Satan as lightning fall from heaven." Luke 10:18.

Question: **Paul, what is he doing here?**

Answer: "But if our gospel be hid, it is hid to them that are lost: in whom the god of this world hath blinded the minds of them which believe not, lest the light of the glorious gospel of Christ, who is the image of God, should shine unto them." 2 Corinthians 4:3, 4.

Question: **How successful has he been?**

Answer: "And we know that we are of God, and the whole world lieth in wickedness." 1 John 5:19.

Question: **Moses, once before, conditions of evil approached this crisis state, did they not?**

Answer: "And God saw that the wickedness of man was great in the earth, and that every imagination of the thoughts of his heart was only evil continually." Genesis 6:5.

Question: **In consequence, what did God purpose to do?**

Answer: "The Lord said, I will destroy man whom I have created from the face of the earth; both man, and beast, and the creeping thing, and the fowls of the air; for it repenteth me that I have made them." Genesis 6:7.

Question: **Just how bad had the situation become?**

Answer: "The earth also was corrupt before God, and the earth was filled with violence." Genesis 6:11.

Question: **Was this the deciding factor in the destruction by the Flood?**

Answer: "God said unto Noah, The end of all flesh is come before me; for the earth is filled with violence through them; and, behold, I will destroy them with the earth." Genesis 6:13.

Question: **Moses, why was Noah saved?**

168

Answer: "Noah found grace in the eyes of the Lord. . . . Noah was a just man and perfect in his generations, and Noah walked with God." Genesis 6:8, 9.

Question: **There is an old spiritual that says, "God gave Noah the rainbow sign. It won't be water but fire next time." Is this true, Malachi?**

Answer: "For behold, the day cometh, that shall burn as an oven; and all the proud, yea, and all that do wickedly, shall be stubble: and the day that cometh shall burn them up, saith the Lord of hosts, that it shall leave them neither root nor branch." Malachi 4:1.

Question: **Malachi, God spared Noah during the Flood. Will He exempt anyone from the fire?**

Answer: "They shall be mine, saith the Lord of hosts, in that day when I make up my jewels; and I will spare them, as a man spareth his own son that serveth him." Malachi 3:17.

Question: **Paul, when may we expect the day of the Lord to come?**

Answer: "The Lord himself shall descend from heaven with a shout, with the voice of the archangel, and with the trump of God: and the dead in Christ shall rise first." "For yourselves know perfectly that the day of the Lord so cometh as a thief in the night." 1 Thessalonians 4:16; 5:2.

Question: **It is perfectly obvious that the "day of the Lord" begins with the second coming of Christ. What will men be doing as that day approaches? Luke, will you answer?**

Answer: "Many shall come in my name, saying, I am Christ." "Men's hearts failing them for fear, and for looking after those things that are coming on the earth." "They shall lay their hands on you, and persecute you." "Ye shall be betrayed both by parents, and brethren, and kinsfolks, and friends." "Nation shall rise against nation, and kingdom against kingdom." Luke 21:8, 26, 12, 16, 10.

Question: **Matthew, what indication have we that crisis-conditioned man in the midst of extreme peril will be doing "business as usual" when Christ comes?**

Answer: "As the days of Noe were, so shall also the coming of the Son of man be. For as in the days that were before the flood they were eating and drinking, marrying and giving in marriage, until the day that Noe entered into the ark. And knew not until the flood came, and took them all away; so shall also the coming of the Son of man be." Matthew 24:37-39.

Question: **How will the righteous greet the coming of the Lord, Isaiah?**

Answer: "It shall be said in that day, Lo, this is our God; we have waited for him, and he will save us: this is the Lord; we have waited for him, we will be glad and rejoice in his salvation." Isaiah 25:9.

Question: **Matthew, describe this dramatic deliverance.**

Answer: "Then shall appear the sign of the Son of man in heaven: and then shall all the tribes of the earth mourn, and they shall see the Son of man coming in the clouds of heaven with power and great glory. And he shall send his angels with a great sound of a trumpet, and they shall gather together his elect from the four winds, from one end of heaven to the other." Matthew 24:30, 31.

Question: **Paul, who will be gathered at that time?**

Answer: "The dead in Christ shall rise first: then we which are alive and remain shall be caught up together with them in the clouds, to meet the Lord in the air: and so shall we ever be with the Lord." 1 Thessalonians 4:16, 17.

Question: **I see. The righteous "rise" and are "caught up" to God. Where do they eventually go, John?**

Answer: "I heard a voice from heaven, as the voice of many waters, and as the voice of a great thunder: and I heard the voice of harpers harping with their harps. . . . These are they which were not defiled with women; for they are virgins. These are they which follow the Lamb whithersoever he goeth. These were redeemed from among men, being the firstfruits unto God and to the Lamb." Revelation 14:2-4.

Question: **So the righteous do go to heaven at the second coming of Christ. Revelation 14:3 says that the music was "before the throne" of God. David, where is God's throne?**

Answer: "The Lord is in his holy temple, the Lord's throne is in heaven." Psalm 11:4.

Question: **That the righteous will enter heaven is now clear. Is that what Jesus meant when He said, "I go to prepare a place for** you. . . . That where I am there ye may be also''? John, how long will the righteous remain in heaven?

Answer: "I saw thrones, and they sat upon them, and judgment was given unto them: . . . and they lived and reigned with Christ a thousand years." Revelation 20:4.

Question: **Paul, what will happen to the wicked when Jesus comes? Will the wicked be expecting the fate that awaits them?**

Answer: "When they shall say, Peace and safety; then sudden destruction cometh upon them, as travail upon a woman with child; and they shall not escape." 1 Thessalonians 5:3.

Question: **Peter, what pleasure will the Lord get from punishing the wicked?**

Answer: "The Lord is not slack concerning his promise, as some men count slackness; but is longsuffering to us-ward, not willing that any should perish, but that all should come to repentance." 2 Peter 3:9.

Question: **Ezekiel, do you agree?**

Answer: "Cast away from you all your transgressions, whereby ye have transgressed; and make you a new heart and a new spirit: for why will ye die, O house of Israel? For I have no pleasure in the death of him that dieth, saith the Lord God: wherefore turn yourselves, and live ye." Ezekiel 18:31, 32.

Question: **This appeal seems to fall on deaf ears. How will the Lord react to human indifference?**

Answer: "Behold, the Lord cometh out of his place to punish the inhabitants of the earth for their iniquity: the earth also shall disclose her blood, and shall no more cover her slain." Isaiah 26:21.

Question: **Isaiah, will you further describe the discomfiture of the wicked at the return of our Lord?**

Answer: "The slain of the Lord shall be at that day from one end of the earth even unto the other end of the earth: they shall not be lamented, neither gathered, nor buried; they shall be dung upon the ground." Jeremiah 25:33.

Question: **How desolate will the earth then be?**

Answer: "I beheld the earth, and, lo, it was without form and void; and the heavens, and they had no light. I beheld the mountains, and, lo, they trembled, and all the hills moved lightly. I beheld, and, lo, there was no man, and all the birds of the heavens were fled.'' Jeremiah 4:23-25.

Question: **But, Jeremiah, what of the beautiful cities that adorn the earth?**
Answer: ''I beheld, and, lo, the fruitful place was a wilderness, and all the cities thereof were broken down at the presence of the Lord, and by his fierce anger.'' Jeremiah 4:26.

Question: **With the righteous in heaven and the wicked dead, it seems that Satan will have nothing to do but reflect on the sorry fate he has brought on the earth. For how long will the wicked rest in death?**
Answer: ''The rest of the dead lived not again until the thousand years were finished. This is the first resurrection.'' Revelation 20:5.

Question: **John, this must be the binding of Satan.**
Answer: ''I saw an angel come down from heaven, having the key of the bottomless pit and a great chain in his hand. And he laid hold on the dragon, that old serpent, which is the Devil, and Satan, and bound him a thousand years.'' Revelation 20:1, 2.

Question: **That is clear. What will happen at the end of the thousand years, John?**
Answer: ''When the thousand years are expired, Satan shall be loosed out of his prison.'' Revelation 20:7.

Question: **When the thousand years are finished, God will resurrect the wicked dead. This is what looses Satan. What will he then do, John?**
Answer: He will ''go out to deceive the nations which are in the four quarters of the earth, Gog and Magog, to gather them together to battle: the number of whom is as the sand of the sea. And they went up on the breadth of the earth, and compassed the camp of the saints about, and the beloved city: and fire came down from God out of heaven, and devoured them.'' Revelation 20:8, 9.

Question: **How can they surround the city on earth when it is still in heaven, John?**
Answer: ''I John saw the holy city, new Jerusalem, coming down from God out of heaven, prepared as a bride adorned for her husband.'' Revelation 21:2.

Question: **So the earth will be purified by fire. Is that right, John?**

Answer: "The sea gave up the dead which were in it; and death and hell delivered up the dead which were in them: and they were judged every man according to their works. And death and hell were cast into the lake of fire. This is the second death." Revelation 20:13, 14.

Thank you, gentlemen, for an enlightening discussion. In a later interview we will discuss hell-fire and the hereafter. The solemn thoughts covered in this lesson are pregnant with spiritual meaning. That each reader will sense this meaning and *run* to Christ for refuge is my prayer.

PAINTING BY JES SCHLAIKJER, N.A.   © BY REVIEW AND HERALD

An exile on the island of Patmos, John in vision was permitted to behold
the glories of heaven, and of man at home in the new earth.

A City Called Heaven

22

A City Called Heaven

Few religions deny the existence of a fairer world than this. Some cling stubbornly to the outmoded theory of making this world a heaven on earth, and all the while uncontrollable forces are at work tearing it apart. The sin of Adam started this world on its plunge downward. Succeeding generations have multiplied the rebellion and its consequences. This planet is rapidly becoming unfit for human habitation.

In spite of human technology, man's problems become more complicated. His inventive genius is turned to militaristic purposes. He is in the strange position of piping the tune that feeds the frenzy of his orgiastic dance of death. This world is doomed. Is there another? Perhaps the prophets have the answer.

Question: **Peter, will there come an end to life on this planet as we now know it?**

Answer: "But the day of the Lord will come as a thief in the night; in the which the heavens shall pass away with a great noise, and the elements shall melt with fervent heat, the earth also and the works that are therein shall be burned up." 2 Peter 3:10.

Question: **Will destruction come because God desires it? Ezekiel, have you a word from God?**

Answer: "I have no pleasure in the death of him that dieth, saith the Lord God: wherefore turn yourselves, and live ye." Ezekiel 18:32.

Question: **Then there is a way of escape. Is there further word from God, Ezekiel?**

Answer: "If the wicked will turn from all his sins that he hath committed, and keep all my statutes, and do that which is lawful and right, he shall surely live, he shall not die.'' Ezekiel 18:21.

Question: **What decided effort must be put forth by every man who would be saved?**

Answer: "Cast away from you all your transgressions, whereby ye have transgressed; and make you a new heart and a new spirit." "Repent and turn yourselves from all your transgressions; so iniquity shall not be your ruin." Ezekiel 18:31, 30.

Question: **Paul, will even a simple majority of sinners obey the above counsel?**

Answer: "But evil men and seducers shall wax worse and worse, deceiving, and being deceived." 2 Timothy 3:13.

Question: **Malachi, how will the rebellion end?**

Answer: "Behold, the day cometh, that shall burn as an oven; and all the proud, yea, and all that do wickedly, shall be stubble: and the day that cometh shall burn them up, saith the Lord of hosts, that it shall leave them neither root nor branch." Malachi 4:1.

Question: **Is there any escape for those who repent of their sins and turn to God? John, what does Jesus say?**

Answer: "Let not your heart be troubled: ye believe in God, believe also in me. In my Father's house are many mansions: if it were not so, I would have told you. I go to prepare a place for you. And if I go and prepare a place for you, I will come again, and receive you unto myself; that where I am, there ye may be also." John 14:1-3.

Question: **Why does Christ have to establish our right to go to heaven or prepare a place for us? David, have you an answer?**

Answer: "The heaven, even the heavens, are the Lord's: but the earth hath he given to the children of men." Psalm 115:16.

Question: **Then Christ, by His priestly ministry, is securing our privilege for heaven. Wonderful! Paul, when will God's people be taken out of the earth?**

Answer: "The Lord himself shall descend from heaven with a shout, with the voice of the archangel, and with the trump of God: and the dead in Christ shall rise first: then we which are alive and remain shall be caught up together with them in the clouds, to meet the Lord in the air: and so shall we ever be with the Lord." 1 Thessalonians 4:16, 17.

Question: **Where will they be taken, John?**

Answer: "They sung as it were a new song before the throne, and before the four beasts, and the elders: and no man could learn that song but the hundred and forty and four thousand, which were redeemed from the earth. . . . These were redeemed from among men." Revelation 14:3, 4.

Question: **So they will be taken where the throne of God is. David, where is that?**

Answer: "The Lord is in his holy temple, the Lord's throne is in heaven: his eyes behold, his eyelids try, the children of men." Psalm 11:4.

Question: **Paul, how many levels of heaven are there?**

Answer: "I knew a man in Christ above fourteen years ago, (whether in the body, I cannot tell; or whether out of the body, I cannot tell: God knoweth;) such an one caught up to the third heaven. . . . How that he was caught up into paradise, and heard unspeakable words, which it is not lawful for a man to utter." 2 Corinthians 12:2-4.

Question: **Moses, give us some idea of the extent of the first heaven. Have you a word from God on this?**

Answer: "God said, Let the waters bring forth abundantly the moving creature that hath life, and fowl that may fly above the earth in the open firmament of heaven." Genesis 1:20.

Question: **So the first heaven is where the birds fly. What about the second?**

Answer: "God said, Let there be lights *in the firmament of the heaven* to divide the day from the night; and let them be for signs, and for seasons, and for days, and years: and let them be for lights in the firmament of the heaven to give light upon the earth: and it was so." Genesis 1:14, 15.

Question: **Isaiah, tell us something of the third heaven.**

Answer: "In the year that king Uzziah died I saw also the Lord sitting upon a throne, high and lifted up, and his train filled the temple." Isaiah 6:1.

Question: **John, what did Jesus call the third heaven?**

Answer: "In my Father's house are many mansions." John 14:2.

Question: **John, are the dead or living saints in heaven now?**

What did Jesus tell Peter?

Answer: "Simon Peter said unto him, Lord, whither goest thou? Jesus answered him, Whither I go, thou canst not follow me now; but thou shalt follow me afterwards." John 13:36.

Question: **When did Jesus say that the saints could follow Him to glory?**

Answer: "If I go and prepare a place for you, I will come again, and receive you unto myself; that where I am, there ye may be also." John 14:3.

Question: **What did the patriarchs, especially Abraham, expect in the third heaven?**

Answer: "He looked for a city which hath foundations, whose builder and maker is God." Hebrews 11:10.

Question: **Paul, what do you think of this?**

Answer: "We know that if our earthly house of this tabernacle were dissolved, we have a building of God, an house not made with hands, eternal in the heavens." 2 Corinthians 5:1.

Question: **Then God *does* have a city out there in space?**

Answer: "Ye are come unto mount Sion, and unto the city of the living God, the heavenly Jerusalem, and to an innumerable company of angels." Hebrews 12:22.

Question: **John, I understand it was your privilege to see the city. Am I correct?**

Answer: "I John saw the holy city, new Jerusalem, coming down from God out of heaven, prepared as a bride adorned for her husband." Revelation 21:2.

Question: **I will come back to you, John, for an eyewitness should be questioned at length. Why is it so necessary that the saints have this city of refuge?**

Answer: "Here have we no continuing city, but we seek one to come." Hebrews 13:14.

Question: **Do you mean that all earthly cities face extinction? Be careful, John, this is a delicate subject.**

Answer: "There were voices, and thunders, and lightnings; and there was a great earthquake, such as was not since men were upon the earth, so mighty an earthquake, and so great. And the great city was divided into three parts, and the cities of the nations fell: and great Babylon came in remembrance before

God, to give unto her the cup of the wine of the fierceness of his wrath." Revelation 16:18, 19.

Question: **Thank God for His city, which is to be our refuge in space! Now, John, you saw it. How did this come about?**

Answer: "There came unto me one of the seven angels which had the seven vials full of the seven last plagues, and talked with me, saying, Come hither, I will shew thee the bride, the Lamb's wife." Revelation 21:9.

Question: **You were invited by an angel! From what vantage point did you see the city?**

Answer: "He carried me away in the spirit to a great and high mountain, and shewed me that great city, the holy Jerusalem, descending out of heaven from God." Revelation 21:10.

Question: **What was the appearance of the city?**

Answer: "Her light was like unto a stone most precious, even like a jasper stone, clear as crystal." Revelation 21:11.

Question: **What of the walls and gates? Who guards them?**

Answer: It "had a wall great and high, and had twelve gates, and at the gates twelve angels, and names written thereon, which are the names of the twelve tribes of the children of Israel." Revelation 21:12.

Question: **If you could read the names written over the gates of the city, you certainly got a good look, John. Do you have anything to add?**

Answer: "The wall of the city had twelve foundations, and in them the names of the twelve apostles of the Lamb." Revelation 21:14.

Question: **John, what about the food?**

Answer: "In the midst of the street of it, and on either side of the river, was there the tree of life, which bare twelve manner of fruits, and yielded her fruit every month: and the leaves of the tree were for the healing of the nations." Revelation 22:2.

Question: **What will be the best experience of all who reach heaven?**

Answer: "There shall be no more curse: but the throne of God and of the Lamb shall be in it; and his servants shall serve him: and they shall see his face; and his name shall be in their foreheads." Revelation 22:3, 4.

Question: **We cannot see God's face, for He is righteous and our human nature would be consumed. But the coming of Christ will change us, won't it, Paul?**

Answer: "Behold, I shew you a mystery; We shall not all sleep, but we shall all be changed, in a moment, in the twinkling of an eye, at the last trump." 1 Corinthians 15:51, 52.

Question: **Will we be able to face Him in person?**

Answer: "Beloved, now are we the sons of God, and it doth not yet appear what we shall be: but we know that, when he shall appear, we shall be like him; for we shall see him as he is." 1 John 3:2.

Question: **John, what promise have we that all will be well thereafter?**

Answer: "God shall wipe away all tears from their eyes; and there shall be no more death, neither sorrow, nor crying, neither shall there be any more pain: for the former things are passed away." Revelation 21:4.

Question: **John, may we trust all these things that you have said to us? Did the angel affirm it?**

Answer: "He said unto me, These sayings are faithful and true: and the Lord God of the holy prophets sent his angel to shew unto his servants the things which must shortly be done." Revelation 22:6.

Question: **John, what have you to say?**

Answer: "I John saw these things, and heard them. And when I had heard and seen, I fell down to worship before the feet of the angel which shewed me these things." Revelation 22:8.

Thank you, gentlemen, for an interesting study. You have fired our hopes, strengthened our faith, and quickened our weary footsteps heavenward. The things of earth are pale beside the vision that you hold before us. And through it all, the love of God stands revealed. Be it forever remembered that "the Lord is not slack concerning his promise, as some men count slackness; but is longsuffering to us-ward, not willing that any should perish, but that all should come to repentance." 2 Peter 3:9.

God has promised eternal life in a perfect world to those who accept Christ's plan for their lives. In that better world our fondest dreams will come true.

The New Earth

23

The New Earth

In our last lesson we learned something of the destruction of the earth. This interview goes into greater detail and covers the final restoration of all things. The ultimate triumph of right over wrong has commanded the attention of philosophers and men of religion in all ages. Occasionally God breaks through to man, asserting His Lordship, sometimes in justice as with the Flood; more often in mercy. In Him, verily, justice and mercy have kissed each other. They are the twin pillars of His character. Some men find it hard to reconcile the two. It is perhaps due to the fact that human nature recoils from retribution. God in His mercy has pulled back the curtain of the future, and we shall need this glimpse of punishment and glory in the trying days ahead.

Question: **Solomon, what dangerous tendency of man jeopardizes his salvation?**

Answer: "Because sentence against an evil work is not executed speedily, therefore the heart of the sons of men is fully set in them to do evil." Ecclesiastes 8:11.

Question: **Can the sinner hope to escape his fate while continuing his wickedness?**

Answer: "It shall not be well with the wicked, neither shall he prolong his days, which are as a shadow; because he feareth not before God." Ecclesiastes 8:13.

Question: **In this life the good seem often to inherit evil and the evil have it easy. Then why do good?**

Answer: "Though a sinner do evil an hundred times, and his days be prolonged, yet surely I know that it shall be well with them that fear God, which fear before him." Ecclesiastes 8:12.

Question: **David, you had this problem. What is your solution?**

Answer: "I have seen the wicked in great power, and spreading himself like a green bay tree." "The wicked have drawn out the sword, and have bent their bow, to cast down the poor and needy, and to slay such as be of upright conversation." "Rest in the Lord, and wait patiently for him: fret not thyself because of him who prospereth in his way, because of the man who bringeth wicked devices to pass." "But the transgressors shall be destroyed together: the end of the wicked shall be cut off." Psalm 37:35, 14, 7, 38.

Question: **What assurance for the righteous have you at this point, David?**

Answer: "The Lord loveth judgment, and forsaketh not his saints; they are preserved for ever: but the seed of the wicked shall be cut off." "Wait on the Lord, and keep his way, and he shall exalt thee to inherit the land: when the wicked are cut off, thou shalt see it." Psalm 37:28, 34.

Question: **You speak of the wicked being cut off, David. What do you mean by this?**

Answer: "The wicked shall perish, and the enemies of the Lord shall be as the fat of lambs: they shall consume; into smoke shall they consume away." Psalm 37:20.

Question: **Malachi, where there is smoke, there is fire. Is that what hell is? The destruction of the wicked?**

Answer: "Behold, the day cometh, that shall burn as an oven; and all the proud, yea, and all that do wickedly, shall be stubble: and the day that cometh shall burn them up, saith the Lord of hosts, that it shall leave them neither root nor branch." Malachi 4:1.

Question: **Isaiah, is this what God wants to do?**

Answer: "The Lord shall rise up as in mount Perazim, he shall be wroth as in the valley of Gibeon, that he may do his work, his strange work; and bring to pass his act, his strange act." Isaiah 28:21.

Question: **So this is distasteful to God, strange to Him; but it is His work. Moses, how does this fit God's character?**

Answer: "The Lord passed by before him, and proclaimed, The Lord, The Lord God, merciful and gracious, longsuffering, and abundant in goodness and truth, keeping mercy for thousands, forgiving iniquity and transgression and sin, and that will by no means clear the guilty." Exodus 34:6, 7.

Question: **After six thousand years of patience, time is running out for the human race. The sinner is hardened in his sins, and God is firmly determined to end it all! Is this true, Isaiah?**

Answer: "Now therefore be ye not mockers, lest your bands be made strong: for I have heard from the Lord God of hosts a consumption, even determined upon the whole earth." Isaiah 28:22.

Question: **What is God's desire for all men? Peter, will you answer?**

Answer: "The Lord is not slack concerning his promise, as some men count slackness; but is longsuffering to us-ward, not willing that any should perish, but that all should come to repentance." 2 Peter 3:9.

Question: **Ezekiel, do you agree? What did God say?**

Answer: "Have I any pleasure at all that the wicked should die? saith the Lord God: and not that he should return from his ways, and live?" Ezekiel 18:23.

Question: **Paul, what indisputable proof have we that God finds punishment distasteful?**

Answer: "When we were yet without strength, in due time Christ died for the ungodly." Romans 5:6.

Question: **John, will you add to this?**

Answer: "God so loved the world, that he gave his only begotten Son, that whosoever believeth in him should not perish, but have everlasting life." John 3:16.

Question: **Did God intend for people to burn in hell?**

Answer: "Then shall he say also unto them on the left hand, Depart from me, ye cursed, into everlasting fire, prepared for the devil and his angels." Matthew 25:41.

Question: **May we escape the fires of hell, Ezekiel?**

Answer: "Therefore I will judge you, O house of Israel, every one according to his ways, saith the Lord God. Repent, and turn yourselves from all your transgressions; so iniquity shall not be your ruin." Ezekiel 18:30.

Question: **Peter, when hell burns, will it be in some special** part of the earth?

Answer: "The day of the Lord will come as a thief in the night; in the which the heavens shall pass away with a great noise, and the elements shall melt with fervent heat, the earth also and the works that are therein shall be burned up." 2 Peter 3:10.

Question: **So hell-fire will cover the earth, and the fire will burn out. Is that correct, Peter?**
Answer: "Seeing then that all these things shall be dissolved, what manner of persons ought ye to be in all holy conversation and godliness." 2 Peter 3:11.

Question: **Malachi, how complete will the destruction of the wicked be?**
Answer: "And ye shall tread down the wicked; for they shall be ashes under the soles of your feet in the day that I shall do this, saith the Lord of hosts." Malachi 4:3.

Question: **David, do you agree that the wicked will not burn on and on eternally?**
Answer: "The wicked shall perish, and the enemies of the Lord shall be as the fat of lambs: they shall consume; into smoke shall they consume away." Psalm 37:20.

Question: **John speaks of the devil being tormented forever and ever. What does he mean? Perhaps you would like to explain this, John.**
Answer: "Death and hell were cast into the lake of fire. This is the second death." Revelation 20:14.

Question: **"This is the second death." So the devil will die. That is clear. The effect of the fire will be permanent. Good! Tell us, Jonah, you made similar use of "for ever," didn't you?**
Answer: "I went down to the bottoms of the mountains; the earth with her bars was about me for ever." Jonah 2:6.

Question: **Jonah, you were in the whale only three days and three nights, so your use of the words "for ever" refers to the effect of the experience rather than its duration. John, who will pronounce upon the wicked the sentence of death?**
Answer: "I saw a great white throne, and him that sat on it, from whose face the earth and the heaven fled away; and there was found no place for them." Revelation 20:11.

Question: **Peter, is this Christ?**

Answer: Men will have to "give account to him that is ready to judge the quick and the dead." 1 Peter 4:5.

Question: **So this is Christ. John, by what are all men judged?**

Answer: "I saw the dead, small and great, stand before God; and the books were opened: and another book was opened, which is the book of life: and the dead were judged out of those things which were written in the books, according to their works." Revelation 20:12.

Question: **John, will sin be forever ended in the flames of hell?**

Answer: "There shall be no more curse: but the throne of God and of the Lamb shall be in it; and his servants shall serve him." Revelation 22:3.

Question: **John, give us one last look at hell.**

Answer: "But the fearful, and unbelieving, and the abominable, and murderers, and whoremongers, and sorcerers, and idolaters, and all liars, shall have their part in the lake which burneth with fire and brimstone: which is the second death." Revelation 21:8.

Question: **Pardon me for insisting, John, but six thousand years of sin and sorrow lead me to ask once again, are you sure that we will never again experience sin or its wages?**

Answer: "God shall wipe away all tears from their eyes; and there shall be no more death, neither sorrow, nor crying, neither shall there be any more pain: for the former things are passed away." Revelation 21:4.

Question: **But for now, Isaiah, what is the Lord's counsel for His saints?**

Answer: "Come, my people, enter thou into thy chambers, and shut thy doors about thee: hide thyself as it were for a little moment, until the indignation be overpast." Isaiah 26:20.

Question: **And what assurance have we, Isaiah, of the ultimate reign of peace?**

Answer: "He will swallow up death in victory; and the Lord God will wipe away tears from off all faces; and the rebuke of his people shall he take away from off all the earth: for the Lord hath spoken it." Isaiah 25:8.

Question: **What appropriate proclamation may then ring out**

echoing the spirit of the new age?

Answer: "Sing, O ye heavens; for the Lord hath done it: shout, ye lower parts of the earth: break forth into singing, ye mountains, O forest, and every tree therein: for the Lord hath redeemed Jacob, and glorified himself in Israel." Isaiah 44:23.

Question: **After the fire, Zechariah, the city of God will descend to the earth. Where will it rest?**

Answer: "His feet shall stand in that day upon the mount of Olives, which is before Jerusalem on the east, and the mount of Olives shall cleave in the midst thereof toward the east and toward the west, and there shall be a very great valley; and half of the mountain shall remove toward the north, and half of it toward the south." Zechariah 14:4.

Question: **What will be the next act in the drama of the future, Isaiah?**

Answer: "Behold, I create new heavens and a new earth: and the former shall not be remembered, nor come into mind." Isaiah 65:17.

Question: **Daniel, will the new creation be a permanent arrangement?**

Answer: "In the days of these kings shall the God of heaven set up a kingdom, which shall never be destroyed: and the kingdom shall not be left to other people, but it shall break in pieces and consume all these kingdoms, and it shall stand for ever." Daniel 2:44.

Question: **What of the righteous? Will they at last live forever, Isaiah?**

Answer: "As the new heavens and the new earth, which I will make, shall remain before me, saith the Lord, so shall your seed and your name remain." Isaiah 66:22.

Question: **Zechariah, what do you know about the new earth?**

Answer: "It shall be in that day, that living waters shall go out from Jerusalem; half of them toward the former sea, and half of them toward the hinder sea: in summer and in winter shall it be." Zechariah 14:8, 9.

Question: **John, can you confirm the prophecy that God will re-create the earth?**

Answer: "I saw a new heaven and a new earth: for the first heaven and the first earth were passed away; and there was no more sea.'' Revelation 21:1.

Question: **Isaiah, some have pictured heaven as a lazy man's paradise. Is this true?**

Answer: "They shall build houses, and inhabit them; and they shall plant vineyards, and eat the fruit of them. They shall not build, and another inhabit; they shall not plant, and another eat: for as the days of a tree are the days of my people, and mine elect shall long enjoy the work of their hands.'' Isaiah 65:21, 22.

Question: **What of the animal kingdom? Will the ravenous beasts be tamed?**

Answer: "The wolf and the lamb shall feed together, and the lion shall eat straw like the bullock: and dust shall be the serpent's meat. They shall not hurt nor destroy in all my holy mountain, saith the Lord.'' Isaiah 65:25.

Question: **What of the lame and the deaf and all the sick, Isaiah?**

Answer: "The eyes of the blind shall be opened, and the ears of the deaf shall be unstopped. Then shall the lame man leap as an hart, and the tongue of the dumb sing.'' Isaiah 35:5, 6.

Question: **What changes will take place in the earth itself?**

Answer: "For in the wilderness shall waters break out, and streams in the desert. And the parched ground shall become a pool, and the thirsty land springs of water: in the habitation of dragons, where each lay, shall be grass with reeds and rushes.'' Isaiah 35:6, 7.

Question: **Finally, how will it be with the saints?**

Answer: "The ransomed of the Lord shall return, and come to Zion with songs and everlasting joy upon their heads: they shall obtain joy and gladness, and sorrow and sighing shall flee away.'' Isaiah 35:10.

Thank you, gentlemen, for this refreshing view of things to come. That right will ultimately triumph gives us courage to endure the perplexities of this present life. How God must love us that He would open to our eyes the vistas of the future for our encouragement now! May His name be praised in every reader's home, now and forever, world without end. Amen!

Conclusion

The prophets have spoken. Their testimony is faithful and true. Like "a light that shineth in a dark place," their words illumine the past, present, and future. Eager eyes that scan the horizon for the first gray trace of dawn are greeted by a flood of light from the sun of prophetic hope. Earth's darkness deepens, but eternal day approaches. The kingdoms of this world will become the kingdom of our Lord and of His Christ, and He shall reign forever and ever. This hopeful picture of the future is traced by the unerring pen of prophecy. May it be for you a wellspring of hope, a source of daily refreshment, a cornerstone of faith, an anchor to secure you against every storm that breaks.